A BELGIAN COOKBOOK

A BELGIAN COOKBOOK
by *Juliette Elkon*

This classic cookbook celebrates the delicious variations found in Belgian cuisine. Each chapter focuses on a specific geographic region and its specialty dishes. Chapters begin with a cultural and culinary introduction to each area, followed by the distinctive recipes that it holds dear.

THE CUISINE OF ARMENIA *available in January 1996* 0-7818-417-5 $14.95pb

THE ART OF BRAZILIAN COOKERY *Dolores Botafogo* 0-7818-0130-3 $9.95pb

THE JOY OF CHINESE COOKING *Doreen Yen Hung Feng* 0-7818-0097-8 $8.95pb

ALL ALONG THE DANUBE *Marina Polvay* 0-7818-0098-6 $11.95pb

THE BEST OF FINNISH COOKING *Taimi Previdi* 0-7818-0284-9 $19.95hc

THE ART OF HUNGARIAN COOKING *Paula Pogany* 0-7818-0202-4 $8.95pb

THE ART OF IRISH COOKING *Monica Sheridan* 0-7818-0454-X $12.95pb

THE ART OF ISRAELI COOKING *Chef Aldo Nahoum* 0-7818-0096-X $9.95pb

THE ART OF PERSIAN COOKING *Forough Hekmat* 0-7818-0241-5 $9.95pb

POLISH HERITAGE COOKERY *Robert and Maria Strybel* 0-7818-0069-2 $29.95hc

THE BEST OF RUSSIAN COOKING *Alexandra Kropotkin* 0-7818-0131-1 $9.95pb

THE BEST OF SMORGASBORD COOKING *G. Simonson* 0-7818-0407-8 $14.95pb

A SPANISH FAMILY COOKBOOK *Juan and Susan Serrano* 0-7818-0193-1 $9.95pb

THE ART OF TURKISH COOKING *Neset Eren* 0-7818-0201-6 $12.95pb

THE BEST OF UKRAINIAN CUISINE *Bohdan Zahny* 0-7818-0240-7 $19.95hc

(Prices subject to change.)

TO PURCHASE HIPPOCRENE BOOKS contact your local bookstore, or write to: HIPPOCRENE BOOKS, 171 Madison Avenue, New York, NY 10016. Please enclose a check or money order, adding $5.00 shipping (UPS) for the first book and .50 for each additional book.

A Belgian Cookbook

by JULIETTE ELKON

HIPPOCRENE BOOKS
New York

First printed in 1958 by Farrar, Straus and Cudahy, Inc.

Hippocrene paperback edition. 1996.

For information, address:
HIPPOCRENE BOOKS, INC.
171 Madison Avenue
New York, NY 10016

Library of Congress Cataloging-in-Publication Data
Hamelcourt, Juliette Elkon.
A Belgian cookbook / by Juliette Elkon
        p.   cm.
Originally published: New York : Farrar, Straus, and Cudahy, 1958
Includes index.
ISBN 0-7818-0461-2
    1. Cookery, Belgian.   I. Title.
TX723.5.B4H25   1996
641.59493—dc20   95-51182
                                                    CIP

Printed in the United States of America.

Foreword

For too long Belgian cooking has been overshadowed by and confused with French cookery. In this book I am attempting to bring out the unique merits, the indigenous character of Belgium's contribution to good eating.

The French, who are fond of Belgian cuisine, refer to it as Flemish cuisine, much as one speaks of Flemish painting, although the men who made it famous came from both the French and the Flemish linguistic parts of Belgium. In fact, a similarity does exist between Flemish painting and cookery. They have in common an opulence, a truculent naïveté which is as distinct from French subtleties as Breughel is from Clouet.

I have assembled these regional dishes over a period of many years, and in our age of vanishing lore have set them down before they become forgotten. Many have been found in out-of-the-way places where I have watched peasant women at work over their ranges or taken notes from innkeepers in obscure villages. Where the soil is rich and pasture abundant we find dishes thick with cream, but in barren country like the Kempen and the Gaume the daily fare is more likely to be jack rabbit no less tastefully prepared. American hunters and fishermen will be particularly interested in recipes like Deer Chops in Gin and Fisherman's Trout, which come from the Ardennes.

Many recipes have come from my brother's old nurse, Liza, now a withered little old lady of 85. When I was growing up, Liza and her husband kept a little grocery store at the other end of the village. I loved to slice the crimson balls of Edam cheese with the big guillotinelike knife; to weigh the honey bread, the rock candy sugar and the dried prunes; to dole out two cents' worth of candy to children smaller than myself. I spent many a happy afternoon rushing from the clean-smelling kitchen to the adjoining shop at the tinkle of the store bell, while Liza stewed pears in coffee for my *goûter* or smeared great *tartines* with *siroop*—a black, thicker-than-molasses syrup obtained from pears.

Mlle. Bellon from Lokeren, the sister of one of our curés, was a source of many fine recipes. At 75 her tiny slenderness was unimpaired by a phenomenal appetite. Mademoiselle possessed a firm ally in Adèle, her nonagenarian maid, who thought nothing of serving six or eight of us four-course dinners with the appropriate wines. When Burgundy finally caught up with Mlle. Bellon she was past 85, and Adèle had died a few weeks earlier after having been taken around Lokeren in an open *calèche* on her 100th birthday.

It was my grandmother who taught me most of these Belgian specialties. As a hostess she was incomparable. Her greatest achievement I think was that she made her friends, her children and thirteen grandchildren feel that sitting down at her dinner table was a truly civilized moment. This was a time not only to fill up on the bounty set before us, but a time to feel alive in all five senses. With intelligent talk and elegant but simple settings it was a leisurely ceremony maturing into the deep emotional satisfaction of something shared. This is as it should be.

Purchase, New York

Contents

Flanders

Tournai, Mons and the Borinage

Liége, Namur and the Ardennes

A BELGIAN COOKBOOK

ℱlanders

FIFTY MILES of white, sandy public beaches grace the Belgian coastline between the estuary of the Schelde and France. The modern resorts and fishing towns offer the best accommodations; casinos and night clubs are never far away. But better still, the bracing English Channel air sharpens a traveler's appetite for the gourmet delights reserved for him at the oyster beds of Blankenberghe, in the unobtrusive restaurants hidden along the picturesque streets of Bruges, Ghent and Kortryk, or along the byroads shaded by trees bent inland by the wind from the sea.

In this rich pastureland where fat, placid cows graze along the canals, where long, low farm buildings stretch along the horizon, veal is milky white and butter has a hazelnut flavor which delicately infuses cream sauces and turns them into a gustatory delight.

The pace of life is slow in this benighted province. There is time for a two-course breakfast. A housewife can sit down for a second cup of coffee at 10 with honey cake perhaps, or raisin bread, and the latest gossip. The main meal in Belgium is at noon. Supper, except in the more worldly homes, is at 6 —simple fare featuring eggs, bread, cheese, *pâtés* or pork sausages. There are but few desserts on the average menu: custards, cookies and all winter long the ubiquitous, shriveled, pungent russet apples so familiar to American farmers two generations removed.

It is a peaceful, deeply religious country where the mystical genius of the people has expressed itself in cathedrals, market halls, public buildings; in a tradition of fine painting more ancient than the French and just as enduring; in the inspired music of César Franck, in the deep but deceptively naïve poetry of Guido Gezelle; in folk songs hauntingly sad as *Twee Koningskinderen*, ". . . two kings' children who held one another so dear . . ."

As well as artistic qualities the people of Flanders have an astuteness, a commercial sense which has made the cities of Bruges and Ghent great trading centers in Medieval Europe and their burghers so wealthy that the king of France, their liege, on a visit cast a jaundiced eye on their velvet and damask robes and was heard to remark sourly that "Here all the burghers are kings"—a remark which in their stubborn spirit of independence they took as a compliment.

From their splendid past many customs and institutions have survived in Flanders. As an awesome testimonial of the 200 years of Spanish domination which racked Flanders with its ruthless Inquisition and spiced its cooking with Spanish saffron, the Penitents' Procession of Veurne remains one of the most curious religious festivals of Europe. Crowds, silenced by the tolling church bells, mass along the sidewalks. With hair shirts under rough-textured robes and heads covered with hoods, men and women from all over Belgium walk barefooted under the burden of heavy crosses over the cobbled streets of the ancient fishing town.

The first Monday after May 2, Bruges gets all decked out with flags and banners for the Procession of the Holy Blood of Jesus, which is said to be preserved in a bejeweled golden casket and to have been brought back from the Crusades by Thierry d'Alsace in 1150. Languid Bruges, a city built almost entirely in the Middle Ages, is the perfect setting for this two-hour-long pageant of religious floats and groups of minstrels afoot and on horseback. Hearing the citizens of Bruges from their balconies and doorsteps call out fervently as the minstrel groups pass, the visitor suddenly feels as if he were living 800 years ago.

This touch of Medieval mysticism in Flanders is balanced by the earthiness of the Breughelian feasts which come after the procession: heaps of black sausage, mace-flavored fish stews, golden platters of rice pudding edged with festoons of brown sugar, *Vlaaien*—the bready, cartwheel-size fruit torten—bittersweet cream-diluted coffee, thick cinnamon-flavored hot chocolate are on all tables. And late into the night the weak, frothy beer from Alost flows in the village cafés.

Of the cafés Beaudelaire once remarked that in Flanders every other house was a pub. These cafés are places where men carry on "men talk" of fishing and crops; cafés are social clubs too, in villages that do not have even a movie house; and of course cafés are places to discuss the sale of livestock. Seldom are they places of drunkenness, and over the chimney mantel one is apt to find embroidered mottoes saying, *"God ziet ons . . .* God sees us . . ." *"Hier Vloekt men niet . . .* Here one does not swear . . .", for this is Flanders and these people are good.

Mushroom Canapés

- *Canapés Ostendaise*

      3 doz. mussels
      3 doz. large mushrooms
      ½ cup chopped parsley and shallots, mixed
      1 tsp. garlic salt
      3 strips bacon, fried and drained (reserve drippings)
      ½ cup dried bread crumbs, more or less
      1 tsp. anchovy paste worked into
      1 tbsp. butter
         Dusting of cayenne pepper

Scrub mussels and wash in large amount of water. Steam in 1 quart water until shells open. Remove the meat. Reserve. Separate the stems and caps of mushrooms and peel caps. Reserve. Chop stems finely with parsley and shallot mixture. Sprinkle garlic salt into it. Crumble bacon and add to mixture. Reserve.

Roll mushroom caps in bacon drippings. Broil until golden in shallow baking pan approximately 3 inches below broiling unit. Stuff caps with stem mixture. Place 1 mussel in each cap. Sprinkle with bread crumbs and dot with anchovy butter. Dust with cayenne. Return to broiler until golden and serve hot. Yield: 3 dozen canapés.

Found Bread

• *Gevondene Brood—Pain Trouvé*

> 4 slices stale white bread, trimmed
> 1½ cups milk (more or less)
> 2 eggs, beaten
> 4 tbsp. butter (more or less)
> ½ cup heavy Béchamel Sauce (see following recipe)
> ¼ cup grated Parmesan cheese
> ¼ cup minced ham
> ¼ cup bread crumbs

Soak bread slices in milk and eggs beaten together.

Melt butter in frying pan. When it sizzles, sauté bread slices on both sides, over medium heat, until crisp.

Mix hot Béchamel, grated cheese and ham until well blended. Spoon over the toast. Sprinkle with bread crumbs and place on cookie sheet. Brown under the broiler and rush to the table. Serves 4.

Béchamel Sauce

• *Sauce Béchamel*

> 2 tbsp. butter
> 2 tbsp. flour
> 1½ cups hot milk
> Pepper and salt to taste
> ½ cup heavy cream

NOTE: above proportions for light cream sauce; for medium sauce use 3 tbsp. butter and flour; for heavy sauce use 4 tbsp. butter and flour.

Over medium heat melt butter in saucepan. Add flour. With a whisk or slotted spoon mix very rapidly, adding milk slowly while sauce thickens and bubbles. When all milk has been added, allow to boil 8 minutes, stirring slowly until thick and about half the liquid has evaporated. Season to taste. Stir in the cream. Taste, correct seasoning. Do not allow to boil again. Keep warm until needed. Yield: 1 cup (more or less).

Important: For fish this sauce is always made with fish stock instead of milk. For white meats use chicken broth instead of milk.

Cheese Torte

· *Tarte au Maton du Mt. de l'Enclus*

> 1 heaping tbsp. butter
> ½ recipe Pâte Brisée (see Index)
> 1 pint cottage cheese
> 1 tbsp. heavy cream
> ⅛ tsp. salt
> 2 eggs

Butter well a 9-inch pie plate and line with rolled-out Pâte Brisée. Make a fluted edging.

Mix cottage cheese, cream, salt and eggs, and beat well together. Fill pastry with this mixture.

Start in cold oven. Turn to 250° and gradually increase heat to 300° over 15-minute period. Continue baking 40 minutes longer.

To remove torte from pan, proceed as for Fruit Torte (see Index). This torte is eaten hot for lunch, with a salad. Serves 6.

Skate Liver Canapés

- *Foies de Raie*

      4 skate livers
      1 tbsp. butter
    12 toast points, hot
         Black pepper to taste

Poach livers in salted water for 6 to 7 minutes depending on size until done. Remove from liquid and drain on absorbent paper.

While still hot place livers in chopping bowl with butter and mash to a paste.

Spread on toast. Dust with freshly ground black pepper and rush to the table, *hot*. Makes 12 appetizers.

Flemish Pork Liver Pâté

- *Pâté de foie à la Flamande*

      1 lb. unsliced bacon, cubed
    2½ lbs. pork liver
      2 bay leaves
     ⅛ tsp. dried thyme
      4 tbsp. chopped onion
      1 clove garlic, crushed
     ½ cup cognac
         Pepper and salt to taste
      4 slices fat back

Place bacon and whole livers in an iron skillet. Cook over slow heat for one hour with bay leaves, thyme, onion and garlic.

Rub through a food mill. Add cognac and correct seasoning. Place in oblong porcelain pâté casserole or in empty coffee cans. Cover with fat back, then with aluminum foil or lids. Place dishes in a pan of water. Bake in hot oven (450°) for 1 hour.

Store in cool place. Will keep as long as layer of fat on top remains undisturbed. Serve as first course or with a salad.

Calves' Brains Fritters

- *Cervelle de Veau au Soleil*

> 3 calves' brains
> 3 cups chicken stock or canned chicken broth
> 2 tbsp. vinegar
> 3 sprigs parsley
> 3 cloves
> 1 clove garlic
> ⅛ tsp. thyme
> 1 bay leaf
> Salt and pepper to taste

BATTER:

> ¾ cup flour
> 1 tbsp. salad oil
> ½ cup dry white wine
> ⅛ tsp. salt

Clean brains by taking out black veins and membranes. Place in lukewarm water and blanch for 10 minutes. Pour off water. Transfer brains to a pot with other ingredients. Bring to a slow boil, reduce heat and poach for 18 minutes. Drain on absorbent paper. Cube brains. Make batter by blending together batter ingredients. Dip cubes of brain in this batter and fry in deep fat (390°).

Serve on toothpicks as appetizers or as a main course around a mound of white rice with a bottled Sauce Diable.

Brain Patties

- *Boulettes à la Cervelle*

  2 calves' brains
  3 cups Court-Bouillon
  Bread crumbs soaked in milk, equivalent to amount of calves' brains
  1 small onion, finely chopped
  ½ cup mushroom stems and pieces, finely chopped
  1 tsp. chopped parsley
  3 egg yolks
  1 whole egg beaten with 1 tsp. oil
  1 cup bread crumbs
  2 tsp. melted butter

COURT-BOUILLON FOR BRAIN PATTIES:

  4 cups light stock
  1 tsp. lemon juice
  4 peppercorns
  ½ onion
  ½ carrot
  Sprig of parsley

Prepare Court-Bouillon by simmering all the ingredients together for 45 minutes in a covered pot. Allow to cool; strain. Clean brains by taking out black veins and membranes. Cook in Court-Bouillon for 18 minutes. Drain and chop finely. Add soaked bread crumbs, onion, mushrooms and parsley. Add egg yolks and make a smooth paste. Divide and pat into flat meat cakes. Dip each patty into the egg beaten with oil and roll in 1 cup bread crumbs.

Place in an ovenproof baking dish. Moisten each patty with melted butter. Cook in a quick moderate oven (375°) until golden brown on both sides, about 20 minutes. Serve very hot with a tomato sauce. Serves 4.

Brain Paste

• *Pâté de Cervelles*

>   1 calf's or lamb's brain
>   3 tbsp. oil
>   Juice of 1 lemon
>   Pepper and salt to taste
>   1 tbsp. chopped onion

Clean brains by taking out black veins and membranes. Poach for 15 minutes in salted water. Cool. Mash with a fork. Add slowly oil and lemon juice. Stir until the paste is firm enough to hold on a fork.

Season with salt, pepper and chopped onion to taste. Spread on melba toast for hors d'oeuvre.

Brain Balls

• *Croquettes de Cervelles*

>   2 calves' brains
>   2 eggs
>   1 egg yolk
>   1 tsp. chopped parsley
>   1 tsp. bread crumbs
>   Pepper and salt to taste

Clean brains by taking out black veins and membranes. Poach brains for 15 minutes in salted water. Mash with a fork, incorporating all other ingredients. Roll into little balls the size of a walnut.

Fry in deep fat (390°). Yield: about 50 balls.

Leek Custard

- *Flamiche Courtraisienne*

    8 leeks trimmed
    1 recipe Sand Torte Pastry (see Index. Omit sugar, substitute 1 tsp. salt.)
    2 cups evaporated milk
    4 eggs beaten with 2 additional egg yolks
      Pepper and salt to taste

Slice leeks. Wash thoroughly under stream of cold water. Boil 15 minutes in salted water.

Meanwhile, line a 10-inch spring form pan with pastry. Bring evaporated milk to a boil. Pour over beaten eggs to make a custard. Season with pepper and salt. Mix drained leeks into custard and pour into pie crust.

Bake 55 minutes at 325° on the lowest shelf of the oven. Serves 6.

First course, buffet or luncheon dish.

Smoked Herring Appetizers

- *Canapés de Harengs Fumés*

    For 1 medium-sized roe,
        1 tbsp. prepared mustard
        ¼ tsp. paprika

Save roe from herring. They will keep for one month in refrigerator. Before a party, poach roe for 5 minutes in boiling water. Drain on absorbent paper. Add prepared mustard and paprika. Spread on melba toast and serve hot.

Leek Soup

• *Soupe aux Poireaux*

> 6 leeks cut in ½-inch lengths
> 2 cups consommé
> 4 medium potatoes quartered
> 1 head Boston lettuce, finely shredded
> ½ cup chopped sorrel or spinach
> ¼ cup chopped fresh chervil or
> 1 tbsp. dried chervil
> ⅛ tsp. dried savory
> Pepper and salt to taste
> 4 tbsp. heavy cream

Wash leeks under stream of cold water, separating leaves to remove mud. Cook for 30 minutes in equal parts consommé and boiling water. Add potatoes. Cook 15 minutes. Add all other ingredients except cream. Taste and correct seasoning. Crush potatoes and serve very hot with 1 tablespoon heavy cream at bottom of each plate. Serves 4.

Turnip Soup

- *Potage aux Navets*

      4 tbsp. butter
      1 small onion, minced
      6 turnips, peeled and quartered
      1 marrow bone
      ½ tbsp. granulated sugar
        Pepper and salt to taste
        Dusting cayenne pepper
      2 tbsp. quick-cooking tapioca

Melt butter in a deep pot and lightly brown onion in it. Add turnips, 6 cups water, marrow bone, sugar, pepper and salt and cayenne. Bring to a boil and sprinkle in tapioca from a spoon. Reduce heat and simmer 1½ hours. Puree through food mill or in electric blender. Taste. Correct seasoning. Bring to a boil and serve with small croutons. Makes 8 cups.

Buttermilk Soup

- *Soupe au Lait Battu*

      4 cups buttermilk
      6 tbsp. flour, diluted in ½ cup milk
      1 cup apples, sliced paper thin
      1 cup prunes, cooked and pitted

Bring buttermilk to a boil in large pot. When it boils add milk and flour mixture, then apples. Stir until soup thickens. Reduce heat, keep stirring for 7 minutes until flour is cooked. Add prunes. Serve dusted with brown sugar. Makes 6 portions.

Flemish Fish Soup

• *Ghentsche Waterzooie*

        2 qts. water
        1 qt. dry white wine
        2 carrots, diced
        1 onion, chopped
        5 sprigs of parsley
      ¼ tsp. mace
        1 bay leaf
        4 cloves
          Pepper and salt to taste
        2 lbs. fish (carp, brill or perch *and* eel)
        6 small lake fish, or 12 smelts
      ½ cup heavy cream

Simmer water, wine, carrots, onion, herbs and seasoning for 20 minutes. Add carp or substitute. Simmer together until fish is cooked. Rub through food mill into kettle. Place the small fish in sieve. Lower sieve into soup and cook until done. Remove fish and reserve. Add cream to soup. Do not allow to boil again.

Serve with thinly sliced round pumpernickel bread sandwiches, well buttered, and place a small whole fish or 2 smelts in each plate. Serves 6 generously. Freezes very well; reheat in double boiler.

Fish and Shrimp Croquettes

• *Croquettes aux Crevettes*

> 3 tbsp. butter
> 3 tbsp. flour
> 1 cup milk
> 1 cup shredded cooked fish
> 1 cup minced shrimp *
> 2 egg yolks
>   Pepper and salt to taste
> 2 tbsp. heavy cream
> 1 tbsp. lemon juice
>   Bread crumbs
> 1 egg lightly beaten with 2 tsp. olive oil

SAUCE:

> 2 cups Béchamel Sauce (see Index)
> ½ cup shrimp pounded to a paste or put through electric blender
> 3 tbsp. butter

Melt butter in saucepan over low heat. Stir in flour. Slowly add milk, stirring vigorously until smooth and thick. Add fish, shrimp, egg yolks, pepper and salt, cream and lemon juice. Remove from fire, Spread in shallow baking dish. Place in refrigerator. Shape into croquettes. Roll in bread crumbs, then in egg mixture, and again in bread crumbs. Fry in deep fat (390°). To hot Béchamel add shrimp, then butter. Serve separately. Serves 4.

* Pink Ostend shrimp are used for this dish but minced American shrimp provide a good substitute.

Halibut Fritters

- *Beignets de Cabillaud*

> 8 small slices halibut, taken from tail of fish
> Juice of 1 lemon
> Pepper and salt to taste

FRITTER BATTER:

> Combine:
>
> 2 cups flour
> 1 pt. light beer

Season the fish with lemon juice and pepper and salt 2 hours ahead of time.

At the very last moment, drain fish on absorbent paper. Dip into batter and fry in deep fat (390°) until golden brown.

Serve with boiled potatoes, cucumber salad and a highly seasoned Béchamel Sauce (see preceding recipe) to which has been added 1 egg yolk and 1 teaspoon lemon juice. Serves 4.

Baked Oysters au Gratin

- *Gratin d'Huîtres*

> 2 qts. shelled oysters
> 2 cups Gratin Sauce (see following recipe)
> ½ lb. cooked and shelled shrimp *

Poach oysters in salted water. Make a Gratin Sauce using the liquid in which the oysters have cooked.

* These are the small pink Ostend shrimp, but minced American shrimp may be used.

Mix shrimps and oysters in the sauce. Pour into a shallow baking dish or individual ramekins and allow to brown lightly at a safe distance from the broiler. Serves 4.

Gratin Sauce

COMBINE:

> 2 cups Béchamel Sauce (see Index)
> 1/4 lb. freshly slivered Switzerland Swiss cheese
> 3 tbsp. dry white wine

Simmer until cheese is melted. Makes approximately 2 cups.

Creamed Mussels

- *Moules à la Poulette*

> 5 qts. mussels
> 2 celery stalks, sliced
> 1 onion, minced
> Pepper and salt to taste
> 2 cups Béchamel Sauce (see Index)
> 1 egg yolk
> 1/4 cup heavy cream
> 1 tsp. chopped parsley

Scrub mussels and rinse them many times in warm water. Place them in a large pot. Add 2 cups water, celery, onion and seasonings. Cover and steam until all shells are open. Remove mussels from shells. Reserve.

To hot Béchamel Sauce, made with the liquor from the mussels, add egg yolk, heavy cream, parsley and the shelled mussels. Rush to the table. Serves 4.

Court-Bouillon

>   Equal parts water and white wine (4 quarts)
>   1   onion, sliced
>   1   clove garlic
>   2   carrots
>   1   small celery stalk
>   ⅛   tsp. powdered thyme
>   2   sprigs parsley
>   1   bay leaf
>   1   clove
>   Salt to taste
> 14   whole peppercorns

Simmer all together for 1 hour before adding fish. This liquid will keep a week in the refrigerator; 1 tablespoon of vinegar is added per quart. It is at its best when used over again. Use it as a fish stock base for sauces to be served with fish or as a basis for fish or shellfish chowders.

Filets of Sole with Spinach

• *Filets de Sole Vert-Pré*

>   1½ lbs. filet of sole
>   Court-Bouillon for fish (see preceding recipe)
>   3   cups leaf spinach cooked and drained
>   4   cups Sauce Mornay (see following recipe)

Roll filets and fasten them with toothpicks. Poach 4 minutes in Court-Bouillon. Remove and drain on absorbent paper. In a buttered ovenproof baking dish or shallow casserole spread out the spinach. On top of it place the filets from which the toothpicks have been removed. Cover with the sauce. Brown lightly under the broiler. Serves 4.

Sauce Mornay

    2 cups Béchamel Sauce (see Index)
    3 egg yolks slightly beaten with
    1 tbsp. cream
    2 tbsp. grated Parmesan cheese
    2 tbsp. butter
    3 tbsp. dry white wine or sherry

Use Court-Bouillon in place of hot milk in the Béchamel Sauce. Bring Béchamel Sauce to boiling point. Remove from heat. Stir in egg yolk mixture and cheese. Incorporate butter.

Makes 2 cups.

Skate with Brown Butter Sauce

• *Raie au Beurre Noir*

    3 lbs. skate
      Court-Bouillon (see Index)

SAUCE:

    ¼ lb. butter
      Pepper and salt to taste
    2 tbsp. wine vinegar
    2 tbsp. capers
    1 tbsp. chopped parsley

Poach skate until flesh is loose from the bones in the thickest part. Remove from liquid. Drain. Keep hot on a deep serving platter.

To make the sauce, place butter in a frying pan over high heat. Add pepper and salt and allow to brown. Remove from heat. Add vinegar, capers and chopped parsley. Pour over fish on serving platter. Serves 4.

Baked Codfish or Halibut, Flemish Style

• *Morue ou Cabillaud à la Flamande*

> ¼ lb. butter
> 8 individual salted codfish steaks soaked overnight *or* 8 halibut steaks
> 2 lemons, peeled and sliced
> 2 onions, sliced
> Pepper and salt to taste
> ⅛ tsp. allspice
> ½ cup dry white wine
> 2 tbsp. bread crumbs *mixed with*
> 3 tbsp. grated Swiss cheese
> 1 tbsp. chopped parsley

Thickly butter bottom of an oblong ovenproof dish. Arrange in it slices of fish, lemon and onions. Season generously with ground pepper and allspice.

Moisten fish with wine. Sprinkle with bread crumb mixture; dot with butter.

Bake uncovered in moderate oven (350°) for 25 minutes. The sauce by this time should be reduced two-thirds.

Serve sprinkled with chopped parsley. Serves 6 generously.

Hare or Rabbit Stew with Raisins

- *Civet à la Flamande*

Start 24 hours ahead

MARINATING LIQUID:

- 2 cups red wine
- ¼ cup olive oil
- 1 cup white wine
- 1 large onion, sliced
- 8 peppercorns, crushed
- 1 bay leaf
- ⅛ tsp. dried thyme
- ⅛ tsp. dried marjoram
- 1 tbsp. brown sugar

HARE OR RABBIT STEW:

- 1 hare or domestic rabbit, cut up (3 to 4 lbs., dressed)
- 4 tbsp. butter (more or less)
- 2 cups consommé *or* stock
  Liquid and seasonings from *marinade*
- 1 tbsp. flour
- 2 tbsp. butter
- ½ cup dried raisins
- ½ cup dried apples
- ½ cup pitted prunes
  Kidneys and liver from hare
- 1 tbsp. chopped parsley

Marinate hare for 24 hours. Dry pieces of marinated hare with paper towel. Sauté in butter until brown. Add consommé and marinating liquid. With a fork, blend flour and butter. Add to sauce and allow to thicken slightly. Add fruit. Cover and simmer for 1½ hours over slow heat. In last 15 minutes add sliced kidneys and liver.

Remove meats, kidneys and fruit to a preheated deep platter, with perforated spoon. Strain liver into sauce. Taste sauce and correct seasoning. Pour over meats and fruit. Sprinkle with chopped parsley and serve at once with a side dish of boiled or mashed potatoes.

Tongue with Raisins

> • *Langue à la Flamande*

>> 1 cup seedless raisins
>> 1 fresh tongue
>> 6 medium onions
>> 4 leeks, halved
>> 8 stalks celery, halved
>> 4 carrots, halved lengthwise
>> 4 potatoes, halved
>> 1 package frozen Brussels sprouts
>> 2 cups Béchamel Sauce made with water in which tongue was cooked (see Index)
>> ¼ cup heavy cream
>> Juice of 1 lemon
>> 1 bouillon cube
>> ¼ cup Madeira or port wine
>> Salt, pepper, nutmeg to taste

Soak raisins in lukewarm water until plump. Boil tongue 1½ hours or until almost tender. Add all vegetables, and keep boiling together for 35 minutes. Remove tongue from liquid, peel and slice; keep warm on a platter. Drain vegetables and arrange on the platter.

To Béchamel Sauce add heavy cream, lemon juice, bouillon cube, wine and drained raisins. Season with salt, pepper and nutmeg to taste. Pour over vegetables and meat. Serves 6.

Chicken Lamme Goedzak

• *Poulet Lamme Goedzak*

   ¼ lb. chicken livers and liver from capon
   2 slices smoked ham or prosciutto
   ½ lb. Italian peperoni *or*
       Spanish Chorizo sausage, diced
   2 cloves garlic
   1 capon (approximately 8 lbs.)
   ¼ lb. soft butter
   1 piece cheesecloth, 6" x 6"
   1 No. 2 can tomatoes, drained
       Giblets from capon
   1 cup chicken broth
   1 cup Béchamel Sauce (see Index)
       Dusting of cayenne pepper
   ½ cup Madeira or Malaga wine
   1 cup mushrooms sautéed in 1 tbsp. butter

Check chicken livers for any trace of gall. Remove carefully. Parboil livers for 3 minutes. Chop coarsely with ham, sausage and one clove of the garlic. Reserve. Wash and dry capon inside and out. Fill cavity with ham-liver mixture. Rub butter into cheesecloth and cover breast of capon with it.

Roast capon in uncovered pan in very hot oven (450°) until done, about 2 hours.

Meanwhile, simmer tomatoes, second clove of garlic and giblets in chicken broth. When capon is almost done, remove giblets, rub tomato sauce through a fine sieve.

Carve capon in chunky pieces. Reserve and keep hot. Place stuffing in bits in bottom of heated serving dish. Remove all fat from drippings. Add 2 tablespoons water to loosen glaze at bottom of the roasting pan; dust with cayenne. Bring to a boil. To this add strained tomato sauce,

Béchamel Sauce and wine. Mix well. Taste and correct seasoning.

Pour half the sauce over meat and stuffing and serve with Saffron Rice (see following recipe), with sautéed mushrooms and remaining sauce. Serves 8.

Saffron Rice

- *Riz au Saffran*

          1 tbsp. butter
          1 cup rice
      1½ cups canned chicken broth or stock
       ½ cup water
       ¼ tsp. Spanish saffron
          Pepper and salt to taste

Melt butter in heavy skillet. Add rice and all other ingredients. Season to taste. Bring to a boil. Reduce heat, cover and allow to simmer for 25 minutes without disturbing. Stir once thoroughly. Add one tablespoon water if necessary. Cover. Serve when rice is tender, dry and fluffy. Serves 4.

Fricasseed Chicken with Meat Balls

- *Kiek met Ballekens*

> 1 roasting chicken
> 2 stalks celery
> 1 onion
> 1 bay leaf
> Sprig of parsley
> ⅛ tsp. ground nutmeg
> ⅛ tsp. powdered thyme

MEAT BALLS:

> 1 lb. ground veal
> 4 slices white bread, trimmed
> 2 eggs, beaten
> ¼ cup top milk
> Pepper, salt and nutmeg to taste

SAUCE:

> 3 egg yolks
> 4 tbsp. cornstarch
> 1 cup heavy cream
> Dusting of cayenne and nutmeg

Place chicken and giblets, but not liver, in a soup pot with vegetables and seasoning. Barely cover with water. Bring to a boil. Reduce heat and poach 50 minutes or until done, depending on size of chicken. Remove some of cooking broth to smaller pot and reserve for meat balls.

Place veal in a mixing bowl. Crumble bread by rubbing it between palms of both hands. Discard big lumps. Add eggs, milk and seasonings with bread crumbs to meat, and mix all together. Roll firmly into small balls the size of marbles. Simmer meat balls in reserved cooking broth for 7 minutes.

Meanwhile, remove skin from chicken. Carve and disjoint bird and place in a deep serving platter along with meat balls. Cover with aluminum foil and keep in a warm oven.

Strain broth, and bring it to a full boil. Mix together egg yolks, cornstarch and heavy cream, and pour this into broth, stirring rapidly with a wire whisk. Allow to thicken without boiling. Taste and correct seasoning, adding cayenne pepper and nutmeg if desired.

Pour sauce over chicken and meat balls. Arrange Steamed Rice (see following recipe) around platter. Traditional vegetables with this are fresh green peas cooked with mushrooms. Serves 6.

Steamed Rice

    2 qts. water
    1 cup rice
    Pepper and salt to taste

Bring water to a boil in a large pot. Add salt. Drop rice into it and boil rapidly for seven minutes.

Drain in a colander. Wash under a stream of cold water. Place colander and rice over boiling water, cover with folded kitchen towel and allow steam from water to soften grains for 15 minutes or until tender, depending on the quality of the rice.

Invert on a platter. Dust with pepper. Serves 4.

Waterzooie

- 1 capon (7 to 8 lbs.)
- 4 tbsp. butter
- 4 leeks
- 8 stalks celery
- 1 carrot
- 1 small onion
- 4 sprigs parsley
- ⅛ tsp. thyme
- ⅛ tsp. nutmeg
- ½ bay leaf
- 4 cloves
- 4 cans chicken broth
- 1 lemon, thinly sliced with rind
- 1 tbsp. chopped parsley
- 4 egg yolks beaten with ¼ cup heavy cream

Rub capon with butter and brown on all sides under the broiler. Place capon with vegetables and seasonings in a flameproof casserole. Cover with chicken broth. Bring to a boil; reduce heat and simmer 40 minutes, or until tender. Remove capon from liquid. Carve and remove skin and bones, saving meat as large pieces; reserve.

Strain liquid. Place over high heat. Add lemon and parsley; stir in egg-cream mixture and allow to thicken slightly, but do not boil. Add pieces of chicken. Serve from tureen with well-buttered slices of German *Kommiesbroot* or cracked wheat, and place a slice of lemon in each plate. Serves 6.

Flemish Capon

• *Chapon Fin*

>1 8 to 10 lb. capon
>1 qt. dry white wine
>1 can beef consommé
>1 marrow bone
>5 peppercorns, crushed
>⅛ tsp. mace, powdered, *or* ¼ tsp. nutmeg
> Salt to taste
>1 tbsp. parsley, chopped
>8 croutons (see following recipe)

SAUCE:

>2 tbsp. butter
>1 medium onion
>¾ cup claret
>1 tsp. grated lemon rind
>1 doz. oysters and their liquor
>2 tbsp. bread crumbs
> Pepper and salt to taste
>1 tbsp. butter

Place capon in a pot, add all ingredients except parsley and croutons and bring to a boil. Season. Reduce heat; poach until tender.

Meanwhile, make sauce. Melt two tablespoons butter, add onion and sauté till golden brown. Add claret, lemon rind, and oysters and their liquor. Reduce heat, simmer five minutes. Add bread crumbs. Allow sauce to thicken. Correct seasoning to taste and finish with butter.

Remove capon from poaching liquid. Cut into serving pieces; place on a hot platter with Saffron Rice (see Index). Pour a little sauce over bird and pour the rest into a sauce-

boat. Sprinkle with parsley and decorate with croutons.
Serves 8.

Croutons

  4 slices white bread
  3 tbsp. butter (more or less)

Trim crusts from bread and cut each slice in two triangles.
Place butter in a skillet and heat to sizzling point. Arrange
bread in the skillet, reduce heat and brown slowly on both
sides until golden, adding more butter when necessary.
Makes 8 triangular croutons.

Veal à la Courtraisienne

 • *Veau à la Courtraisienne*

  1 beef shank bone
  4 lbs. standing rump of veal
  1 small onion
  1 carrot
  2 celery stalks
  1 bay leaf
 ⅛ tsp. powdered thyme
 ⅛ tsp. ground nutmeg
  4 cloves
   Pepper and salt to taste
  1 cauliflower, large

SAUCE:

  3 egg yolks
  4 tbsp. cornstarch
  1 cup heavy cream
  1 tbsp. lemon juice

Place meats in a soup pot with onion, carrot, celery and seasonings. Barely cover with water. Bring to a boil. Reduce heat; simmer 1 hour 20 minutes or until done. Keep meats warm in juices.

Meanwhile, boil cauliflower 10 minutes in salted water. Pour off the water and replace with some of the meat juices. Boil another 10 minutes, or until tender. Drain broth from cauliflower back into the meat pot. To keep cauliflower warm, place it in a colander over an empty cooking pot and cover.

Remove veal from pot. Slice it and place in a deep serving platter. Surround with pieces of cauliflower. Cover and keep warm in very slow oven.

To make sauce, strain meat broth, discarding shank. Bring broth to a full boil. Mix together egg yolks, cornstarch and heavy cream, and pour mixture into broth, stirring rapidly with wire whisk. Allow to thicken without boiling. Taste and correct seasoning. Add lemon juice.

Pour sauce over meat and vegetable. Serve with boiled, parsleyed potatoes. Serves 6.

Veal Tails

• *Queues de Veau*

 1 head cabbage, quartered
 8 slices bacon
 2 veal tails, cut up *
 2 cups stock *or* canned chicken broth
 ½ bay leaf
 2 cloves
 1 small onion
 ⅛ tsp. powdered thyme
  Pepper and salt to taste

* 1 oxtail may be substituted.

Blanch cabbage 15 minutes in boiling water. Drain thoroughly. Wrap each piece of cabbage in 2 slices of bacon and tie with a string. Place cabbage rolls and veal tails in flameproof casserole. Cover with stock; add 1 cup water, onion and seasonings. Bring to a boil. Reduce heat and allow to simmer 1 hour. Taste and correct seasoning. Serves. 4.

Bruges Stew

- *Ragoût Brugeois*

(Lamb, Veal or Beef)

   3 lbs. stew meat
  ⅛ tsp. powdered thyme
  1 bay leaf
  1 clove
    Salt and pepper
  ½ clove garlic
 12 shallots *or* 1 medium onion, minced
 12 raw carrots in 1-in. chunks
  4 quartered potatoes
  ½ cup chopped celery
  1 tbsp. butter creamed with 1 tbsp. flour
  ½ lb. mushrooms (field mushrooms are best)
  1 tsp. lemon juice
  1 tsp. chopped parsley

Place meat in flameproof casserole. Barely cover with water. Add seasonings, onions, carrots, potatoes and celery. Bring to a boil, cover, reduce heat and simmer 40 minutes (veal, only 35 minutes).

Remove meat to heated dish. Strain juices. Bring to a boil and add butter-flour mixture; allow to thicken and boil 5 minutes over high heat. Reduce heat. Replace meat in pot. Add sliced mushrooms, lemon juice and parsley. Simmer together 15 minutes. Serves 6.

Lamb Chops Uylenspiegel

• *Côtes d'Agneau à l'Uylenspiegel*

> 4 double loin lamb chops, boned
> 4 pork sausages (*boudin blanc,* really)
> 2 large oranges, peeled and sliced
> 4 anchovy filets
> 4 black olives
> 1 cup rich stock *or* canned beef broth

Wrap lamb chops around sausages and fasten with skewers. In the bottom of a shallow baking dish spread orange slices. Place meats on top. On each chop place 1 filet of anchovy wrapped around an olive. Pour stock over all and bake in hot (400°) oven 12 minutes. Reduce heat to 325°. Cover with foil and continue baking for 35 minutes. Remove foil. Brown chops under broiler before serving. Serves 4.

Serve with buttered beets and baked potatoes.

Roast Loin of Pork

- *Rôti de Porc*

    1 10-rib pork loin
    6 green apples
    6 medium potatoes, peeled
    6 large Spanish onions
    1 cup Belgian cider *
    2 tbsp. butter creamed with 2 tbsp. flour
      Pepper and salt to taste

Rub loin with 2 tablespoons salt. Place in large roasting pan. Dust with freshly ground pepper and roast uncovered for 2 hours at 350°. Peel apples halfway and core them. Alternate 1 apple, 1 potato and 1 onion around meat and roast 1 hour longer.

Carve meat. Place it on heated platter with vegetables. Pour off the fat in the roasting pan, place pan over high heat. Add 1 cup boiling cider and butter-flour mixture. With a whisk or spoon blend and mix with pan glaze and drippings. Taste and correct seasoning. Serve gravy from a sauceboat. Serves 6.

* Belgian cider is hard. For same effect substitute ¾ cup cider, ¼ cup apple-jack or brandy.

Sheep's Tongues with Mushrooms

• *Langues de Moutons Forestière*

　　1　15-oz. jar sheep's tongues
　　¼　cup dry white wine
　　6　tbsp. butter
　　¼　tsp. grated onion
　　½　bay leaf
　　⅛　tsp. thyme
　　1　lb. mushrooms, sliced
　　1　clove garlic, grated or pressed
　　　　Pepper and salt to taste
　　1　tsp. parsley, chopped

Slice tongues lengthwise ¼-inch thick. Place them in a flameproof casserole with white wine, 3 tablespoons of the butter, onion, bay leaf and thyme. Simmer 10 minutes.

Meanwhile, in a frying pan sauté mushrooms 5 minutes with remaining butter, garlic, pepper and salt. Add mushrooms to tongues. Taste and correct seasoning. Simmer 15 minutes, covered. Sprinkle with parsley and serve from casserole. Serves 4, generously.

Flemish Black Sausage

• *Boudin des Flandres*

Add to Black Sausage recipe (see Index):

　　¼　cup brown sugar
　　¼　cup seedless grapes⎫ washed
　　¼　cup Smyrna grapes⎭ and well-drained

Serve medium-broiled, with applesauce.

Red Cabbage

- *Chou Rouge*

      3 slices of bacon
      1 medium head red cabbage, shredded
      2 cups water
      2 tbsp. honey
      3 tbsp. currant jelly
      1 tbsp. brown sugar
      1 apple, peeled, cored and sliced
      1 bay leaf
        Pepper and salt to taste
      2 tbsp. honey vinegar *or* cider vinegar
        Dash of cayenne pepper

Line bottom of Dutch oven or flameproof casserole with bacon, add cabbage and other ingredients except vinegar and cayenne. Bring to a boil. Reduce heat and simmer for 2 to 3 hours or until soft. Watch liquid. Add water if necessary so it will not stick. Finish with vinegar, dust with cayenne and serve with pork chops. Serves 4.

Creamed Escarole

- *Endives à la Crème*

      2 large heads escarole
      2 cups Béchamel Sauce (see Index)
      1 tbsp. lemon juice
    ¼ cup heavy cream
        Pepper, salt, nutmeg to taste
      2 egg yolks

Detach leaves of escarole and cut them into pieces 2 inches long. Wash. Place in a pot with a large amount of boiling water. Allow to boil for 15 minutes, drain, and cool to the point when water can be squeezed out of the vegetable by hand.

In the meantime, prepare a Béchamel Sauce, add to it lemon juice, heavy cream and seasonings to taste. Remove from fire and, stirring quickly, blend egg yolks into sauce. Add drained escarole. Loosen vegetable with a fork, mix well with sauce. Reheat over low heat, uncovered.

Serve with any roast or sautéed meat. Serves 4.

Rice Custard

- *Rystpap*

> 3 cups milk
> ⅔ cup packaged precooked rice
> 1 inch vanilla bean
> 4 egg yolks
> Brown sugar

Bring milk to a boil over high heat. Place rice in top of double boiler and stir in boiling milk. Add vanilla bean. Allow to cook over hot water 1 hour. Stir in egg yolks. Cook three minutes. Remove from heat and take out vanilla bean. Spread on dessert plates. Chill. Just before serving sprinkle with brown sugar. Serves 4.

Quick Gaufrettes

- *Gaufrettes Rapides*

  4½ cups all-purpose flour
  ½ cup granulated sugar
  1 tsp. cinnamon
  2 tsp. baking powder
  ¾ lb. sweet butter, softened
  4 eggs
  2 tbsp. rum

In a large bowl sift dry ingredients. Make a well in the center and place butter, eggs and rum in the well. Gradually incorporate all the flour into the other ingredients.

Allow this paste to stand for 2 hours, uncovered, at room temperature. Divide into little balls the size of 2 tablespoons. Cook in waffle iron. Cool on rack and store like a cookie. Makes 3 to 4 dozen.

Wafer Cookies

- *Gaufrettes de Courtrai*

  4½ cups all-purpose flour
  1 tsp. cinnamon
  1 tsp. salt
  1 package dry yeast diluted in ¼ cup lukewarm water
  ¾ cup granulated sugar
  4 eggs
  ¾ lb. butter, softened

In a large bowl sift flour with cinnamon and salt. Make a well in the center and place in it diluted yeast, sugar and eggs. With the fingers gradually incorporate the flour from the sides into the other ingredients until a smooth paste is obtained. Knead well. Place in a buttered bowl and allow to rise in a warm place until double in bulk (2 hours).

Punch down. Incorporate butter into this mass. Divide into balls the size of 2 tablespoons. Place on a baking sheet, cover with a light towel and allow to rise for 1/2 hour.

Bake in a waffle iron. Cool on a rack and store like a cookie. Makes 5 to 6 dozen.

These are always served to New Year's callers with a glass of tawny port.

Filled Wafers

- *Galettes Fourrées*

> 2 doz. gaufrettes (see preceding recipe)
> Colored sugar

FILLING: Kirsch Flavored Butter Cream

> 1 cup granulated sugar
> 1 cup water
> 1/4 lb. sweet butter
> 2 tbsp. confectioners' sugar
> 1/4 cup kirsch *
> 3 egg yolks

Boil sugar and water together until syrup makes a thread when dropped from a spoon (220°). Meanwhile, partially cream butter with sugar and kirsch. Place egg yolks in a bowl and beat syrup into them, slowly at first. Then add partially creamed butter-sugar-kirsch mixture and beat all together until light and fluffy and almost white.

* Rum, strong coffee or 1 teaspoon vanilla extract may be substituted for kirsch, if desired.

Place filling between two gaufrettes, allowing some of the butter cream to show at the edges. Roll edges in colored sugar. Wrap in aluminum foil and store in refrigerator or freezer. Will keep indefinitely. Store at room temperature 2 hours before serving.

Serve for tea or when drinking port or sherry. Makes 1 dozen galettes fourrées.

Lost Bread

- *Verlorene Brood—Pain Perdu*

    3 eggs
    2 cups milk (more or less)
       Vanilla, bourbon or rum
    4 Holland rusks
    4 tbsp. butter (more or less)
    4 tbsp. brown sugar

Beat eggs and milk together. Flavor according to taste with vanilla, bourbon or rum. Pour into 4 soup plates to insure even soaking. Put a rusk in each soup plate and soak for a few minutes.

Heat half the butter in frying pan until it sizzles. Fill pan with one layer of rusks and remaining liquid and sauté as for a crêpe. To turn, put a plate over the rim of the frying pan and invert pan so rusks fall onto plate. Add remaining butter to pan and slide rusks, uncooked side down, from the plate into the pan. Cover top with brown sugar while underside browns. Serve hot. Serves 4.

The rusks can be replaced by bread, but the latter does not have the same finesse.

Puff Pastry

- *Pâte Feuilletée*

    1 lb. sweet butter
    4 cups all-purpose flour
    1 tsp. salt
    1 cup ice water (more or less)

Have rolling pin chilled. Chill it several times during working time.

Wash pastry board or enamel-topped table with ice, then dry.

Take a pound of sweet butter, knead and squeeze it in a bowl of ice water until smooth and waxy. Place it in a cloth and press out any water trapped in it. Press it down into a flat oblong shape about 1 inch high. Sift into a mixing bowl 4 cups all-purpose flour with 1 teaspoon salt. With the finger tips work into the dry ingredients 2 tablespoons of the butter patty. Gradually add *about* 1 cup ice water and with the hands mix quickly and lightly to make a dough about the same consistency as the butter, firm but not hard. Flour lightly working surface of the pastry board or enamel table. Place dough on it, roll it out into a rectangle ¼-inch thick. Place the cake of butter onto it in center of the dough. Fold 1 flap of dough to cover the butter and the second flap of dough over the upper flap making 3 layers and completely covering the butter. Press the side edges of the dough together and chill in refrigerator for 20 minutes. Chill your table top again. Flour it. Place the chilled dough on working surface, roll it into another long rectangle. Roll it as thinly as possible without letting much of the butter break through. Fold the rectangle of dough into thirds and turn it so that one of the side edges faces you. This rolling and folding is called a turn. Make another turn, then chill the dough for 20 minutes. Make 2 more turns and chill again. Make 2 final turns and chill for 15 minutes before rolling and cutting the dough for baking.

Bruges Knots

- *Noeuds de Bruges*

> 1 recipe Puff Pastry (see preceding recipe)
> 1 tbsp. granulated sugar *or,* preferably, fine grain rock candy sugar

Roll out Puff Pastry on floured board to a thickness of ½ inch. Cut into strips ½ inch wide and 10 inches long. Tie strips into loose, simple knots. Moisten with pastry brush dipped in water. Sprinkle with sugar.

Place on heavy baking sheet and bake in moderate oven (350°) 6 to 8 minutes. Keep in airtight container between layers of waxed paper. Makes about 36 knots.

Fruit Torte

• *Vlaaien*

Start 1 day ahead

> 3 cups sour pitted cherries, well-drained (prune compote *or* thinly sliced apples may be used)

BOTTOM CRUST PASTRY: *Pâte Brisée*

> 2 cups sifted all-purpose flour
> 1¼ tbsp. sugar
> 1 tsp. salt
> ⅓ cup cold water
> 1 egg yolk
> ¼ lb. butter

Place flour in a heap on pastry board or table. Make a well in center. Put sugar, salt, water and egg yolk in this well. Press butter through fingers to crumble it, and drop onto other ingredients.

Then with tip of finger start working the flour into other ingredients. Work in a circular motion, gathering flour to the center, mixing all the time, picking up stray bits of flour and butter until sticky ball is formed.

Break off bits of dough, flatten out with palm of hand until entire ball is broken up. Form back into a ball. Repeat process twice. Store overnight in refrigerator for best results.

Punch down dough. Divide into two loaves, one larger than the other. Roll out larger loaf with rolling pin to ¼-inch thickness. Line well-greased 9-inch pie dish with pastry; avoid stretching. Trim overhanging edge to ½-inch with scissors. Prick with fork to avoid puffing during baking.

Fill with cherries, prune compote or thinly sliced apples.

Roll out smaller part of dough and cut into strips ½ inch wide. Lay some of strips one way across filling, about one inch apart. Then place same number of strips diagonally across. Seal ends to pastry on edge of pan with a little water. Turn overhanging pastry back over ends of lattice strips and build up a fluted edge.

Brush pastry with cold water. Bake in slow oven (300°) 45 minutes. To take out of pan, allow torte to stand a few minutes until it shrinks from sides of the pan. Then, with a spatula carefully loosen torte at one side, and holding the pie dish tipped, turn it around to let the air in all around the torte. Allow to cool on wire rack.

Honey Cake

* *Ghentsche Peperkoek*

> 2½ cups all-purpose flour
> ½ cup rye flour
> 1½ tsp. baking soda
> 2 tsp. double-acting baking powder
> 1½ cups lukewarm honey
> ¼ cup water

Blend all ingredients together in a bowl until a smooth, semistiff dough is formed. Place in a well-buttered bread pan. Bake at 275° for 1½ to 2 hours without opening oven door. Test cake with pastry wire: if it comes clean from center of cake it is done.

Allow cake to stand at least one day before use. Serve sliced, buttered and make into a sandwich with a thin slice of white bread. Keeps indefinitely wrapped in foil.

Recipe may be doubled or tripled, if desired.

Antwerp and the Kempen

Anvers et la Campine

ANTWERP, despite its modern trappings, is a Renaissance metropolis. The cathedral, the first stock exchange, with its little courtyard elaborately paved in the varicolored cobblestones of the Portuguese manner, the sumptuous Town Hall, the guild and corporation houses, the fancy doorways and arches which one suddenly discovers in commonplace streets—all point to the fact that before 1570 Antwerp was the most important town in the Lowlands and had a population of more than 100,000.

This was a population alert, cosmopolitan, slightly radical, somewhat irreverent and, at its highest level, patrician, cultured and public-spirited. The magnificent Plantin-Moretus Museum, once the town house of Christopher Plantin the master printer, has been restored to its 16th century splendor. Several generations of Plantins made rich by their diamond works lived there—a dynasty of artistic printers who produced such magnificent books as the famous Polyglot Bible. There too may be seen the famous presses on which so many incunabula were printed as well as portraits done by Rubens of various members of that remarkable family.

The mansion where Rubens lived and of which he was the architect is not far from there. Today it is open to visitors. Anyone may walk in the garden, under the archway used as background for "The Meeting of St. Ambrose and Emperor Theodosius" and share the paths trodden by Isabella Brant and Hélène Fourment, the painter's loves. Anyone may admire the exquisitely contrived vistas which adorn so many of the canvases of one of the most versatile geniuses of the Renaissance.

Antwerp has fine restaurants where the best cosmopolitan food is served in the French manner.

On a sunny day visitors climb to the top of Antwerp's only skyscraper, the Boeren Toren, which was built with funds from a farmer's union. Here one may look seaward to 47 miles of the most modern port installations in Europe and to a gleaming expanse of freight yards, then far beyond, past the fertile strip of reclaimed land known as the Polder to the moorlands of the Kempen which alternate with stretches of pine woods and heath.

The Kempen is a romantically desolate place. Until 1926 only two cobblestone roads went from the larger villages to the market towns of Mol, Hoogstraeten and Herenthals, meandering through the double row of red brick one-storied houses of an occasional hamlet or past the quiescent Abbey of Averbode or the magnificent 15th century Church of St. Dympne at Gheel. There is no pastureland, but near the old Roman burg which is now Tongeren magnificent orchards furnish most of the fruit used by English jam and preserve concerns. The sandy soil, covered with a mass of purple and gold when the heather and the broom are flowering, was good only for the cultivation of asparagus and potatoes. The thatched, isolated farm had no barn, only a hayloft; and in a lean-to, there was a pig. Around the yard a few chickens foraged, and tied to a stake a little goat fed on whatever she could.

This in some places of the Kempen is still the picture today. But since 1926, with the discovery of the rich coal deposits at Winterslag, company towns have sprung up, peopled with Italian and Polish miners. Cement roads have replaced the sand paths once impassable to the automobile, and with progress amusement parks for the workers have been built as well as modest villas and delightful inns. The young women have discarded the kerchiefs, the long skirts and the pretty, flowered bonnets they wore to Mass on Sundays. Frizzy permanents and short dresses have taken the place of the old elegance. Bicycles take the modern girls to work at the canning factories farther south.

At the very southern edge of the Kempen lies the fertile land black with silt from the river Dyle. Here the farmers have from time immemorial dredged the river and, rotating their crops, spread one-fourth of their precious acreage with the organically rich river deposits leaving the fertilized land fallow for a season. This foresighted practice has paid off: the tiny Belgian carrots so highly priced in the U.S., the midget peas, the one-bite stringless beans, the baby onions, the tender lettuce and the giant, glistening cauliflowers are grown here. Very little of this fancy produce is consumed by the owners of these truck garden farms. The people of the Kempen live on simpler things: the big eels that slither from one irrigation ditch to another, the cottontail and the jack rabbit, the blackbird, the scrawny chicken's egg and the cockerel and the horse that have endured beyond usefulness

—all seasoned and garnished with old-fashioned pot herbs.

I have eaten, on Lenten days, Buttermilk Soup and *Knib-bekes Torte* for supper in my grandmother's kitchen. I have enjoyed Poacher's Stew at many a cottage down in the woods and been regaled with Pears Stewed in Coffee by my brother's old nurse. I have walked to the other end of the village to dip a crusty piece of bread in the sauce of an *Estouffade Chevaline* at the house of Liske Block, our local midwife.

A guest at many Kempen weddings, I have, in Breughelian peasant cottages, feasted on eel pie, eaten great chunks of kid or suckling pig roasted on the most primitive of spits but suffused with the fragrance of applewood and pine needles, the crackling skin a golden seal for the juices, its rosy cavity filled with a bunch of herbs. These have been delights I can never forget—the smells and soft contours of the heath on such a night, the glow of the barbecue pits, the stomping dancers, the beery notes of the local trombone and the warmth and gay truculence of these, my people.

Buttermilk Soup

- *Soupe au Lait Battu*

    1 pt. milk
    2 tbsp. flour diluted in 1 cup cold milk
    1 qt. buttermilk
    2 egg yolks, beaten
    Brown sugar to taste

Bring milk to a boil. Add milk-flour mixture and allow to thicken, stirring all the time. Add buttermilk slowly. Bring to a boil. Remove from heat.

Place egg yolks in heated soup tureen. Pour soup over the eggs, stirring all the while.

Add brown sugar at the table. Serves 6.

Milk Soup Wafers

- *Mastellen*

  3 eggs
  1 tbsp. melted butter
  ¼ tsp. salt
  1⅔ cups all-purpose flour (about)
  ½ tsp. baking powder
  2 tsp. coarse granulated sugar

Beat eggs well. Add remaining ingredients except coarse sugar. Knead until smooth (about 5 minutes). Roll out about ⅛ inch thick on floured board. Cut in 4-inch round shapes. Sprinkle with coarse sugar and bake on greased cookie sheet in quick moderate oven (375°) 30 minutes, or until light brown. Serve with Buttermilk Soup (see Index). Makes 6 to 8 wafers.

Asparagus and Potato Soup

- *Soupe aux Asperges*

  1½ lbs. asparagus
  3 medium-sized potatoes
  2 cups consommé *or* stock
  1 tbsp. butter
  2 egg yolks
  ½ cup heavy cream
     Pepper and salt to taste
     Dusting of nutmeg

Clean asparagus, reserving 10 to 12 tips which are to be cooked separately. Cook asparagus with potatoes and consommé and 6 cups water until very soft. Rub through food mill or strainer. Bring to a boil and remove from fire. Add butter, egg yolks beaten in heavy cream. Taste and correct seasoning.

Garnish with reserved cooked asparagus tips. Serve dusted with nutmeg in individual cups or from tureen. Serves 6.

A Superb Cream of Asparagus Soup

• *Crème d'Asperges*

> 2 lbs. asparagus cooked and puréed
> 1½ cups Béchamel Sauce (see Index)
> 1½ cups consommé *or* stock
> 1 cup heavy cream
> 2 tbsp. butter
> 2 egg yolks, beaten

Mix asparagus purée and hot Béchamel. Add consommé. Bring to a boil. Add heavy cream. Bring again to boiling point but do not boil. Remove from heat. Finish with butter and egg yolks, stirring with wire whisk. Makes 6 cups.

Asparagus from Malines

• *Asperges à la Flamande*

> 2½ lbs. white asparagus
> 8 hard-cooked eggs
> 1 tsp. chopped parsley
> ½ lb. butter
> ½ tsp. lemon juice
> Pepper and salt to taste

Peel asparagus. Leave full length. Boil 5 minutes upright, with tips up, in an uncovered pot. Then cook whole asparagus 15 minutes more. After they are cooked add salt, lightly. Drain.

Serve on a porcelain rack or a folded napkin surrounded by halves of hard-cooked eggs and chopped parsley. On the side serve melted butter to which lemon juice has been added.

Eggs are mashed with butter sauce and parsley on the plate and the tip of the asparagus is dipped into the mixture while left hand holds end of vegetable. Tricky, but essential.

Serves 4 for a main dish, 6 as a first course.

Early June Peas

• *Petits Pois au Pourpier*

```
  2 pts. early June peas
 ¼ lb. butter
  1 cup washed and drained purslane leaves
 ½ cup water
  2 tsp. granulated sugar
  1 tbsp. finely chopped parsley
    Pepper and salt to taste
  2 egg yolks, beaten
```

Place peas in casserole with butter, purslane, water, sugar and parsley. Simmer until tender. Season to taste and add egg yolks. Stir gently until thickened. Serves 6.

Purslane *

- *Pozellaen*

>   2 lbs. purslane
>   2 tbsp. butter
>   Pepper and salt to taste
>   1 egg yolk

Take the tips and leaves of purslane. Blanch in boiling salted water. Drain. Place in a casserole with butter, pepper and salt, and egg yolk. Stir continuously. Heat and serve. Serves 4.

Oyster Plant Fritters

- *Beignets de Salsifis*

>   1 lb. oyster plant
>   1 tsp. vinegar

BATTER:

>   1 cup flour
>   1 cup light beer
>   ⅕ tsp. salt

Scrub oyster plant like a carrot, until it is white. Cut into pieces two inches long. Rinse in cold water. Parboil 12 minutes in 2 quarts boiling water to which vinegar has been added. Drain on absorbent paper.

Combine batter ingredients and mix well with a spoon. Roll each little oyster plant stick in the batter and fry in deep fat until golden brown.

Serve very hot. Serves 4.

* Purslane, considered by most gardeners a weed, is a succulent pot herb. The bigger leaves picked from the stems before flowering are often served in Belgium in chicken noodle soup too.

Cauliflower Fritters

Substitute florets of raw cauliflower for oyster plant in preceding recipe.

Mushrooms Fines Herbes au Gratin

* *Champignons*

    2 lbs. fresh mushrooms (chanterelles are the best)

MARINATING LIQUID:

    ½ cup salad oil
    1 tbsp. grated onion
    1 tbsp. chives, minced
    1 tbsp. parsley
    1 tsp. dried chervil
    ¼ tsp. dried tarragon
    ¼ tsp. dried thyme
    Dusting of cayenne
    3 tbsp. vinegar
    1 clove garlic, pressed
    3 tbsp. butter
    1 cup Gratin Sauce (see Index)
    ½ cup bread crumbs

Slice mushrooms and firm part of stem. Marinate for 2 hours in above liquid. Pour liquid from mushrooms. (Reserve marinating liquid for the next time or incorporate some of it in salad dressings. It will keep 2 or 3 weeks in refrigerator.)

Sauté mushrooms in butter over high heat for 2 minutes. Lower heat and continue cooking, stirring now and then, until tender (about 7 minutes). Transfer contents of pan to shallow baking dish. Cover with sauce and sprinkle with bread crumbs. Brown under the broiler and serve at once. Serves 4.

Cabbage or Cauliflower Au Gratin

- *Chou ou Choufleur*

    3 lbs. shredded cabbage or cauliflowerets
    ½ cup grated Parmesan cheese
    1 cup Béchamel Sauce (see Index)
    ¼ cup white wine
    2 tbsp. bread crumbs
    1 tsp. butter

Steam shredded cabbage in boiling salted water for about 15 minutes. Drain carefully. Melt cheese in Béchamel Sauce. Add white wine. Arrange cabbage in casserole. Pour cheese sauce over it and mix it in with wooden spoon. Sprinkle with bread crumbs; dot with butter and bake in very hot oven (475°) just long enough to brown bread crumbs.

For a main course, add diced beef, ham or tongue to sauce. Serve piping hot and have a crisp salad on the side. Serves 6.

Creamed Oyster Plant

- *Salsifis à la Crème*

    1 lb. oyster plant
    1 tsp. vinegar
    2 cups Béchamel Sauce (see Index)
    2 egg yolks, beaten
    1 tbsp. lemon juice

Scrub oyster plant like a carrot until it is white. Cut into pieces 2 inches long. Rinse carefully in cold water. Parboil 20 minutes in 2 quarts water to which vinegar has been added.

Drain and serve in Béchamel Sauce to which egg yolks and lemon juice have been added just before serving. Serves 4.

Cabbage and Potato Casserole

- *Stoemp mé Spek*

       1 medium-sized head of cabbage
       5 large potatoes
       ⅛ tsp. grated nutmeg
       ⅛ tsp. pepper
       1 lb. lean bacon

Chop cabbage and boil with the potatoes in a pot for about 40 minutes; salt according to taste.

Mash all together. Heat in an earthenware pot with nutmeg and pepper. Dice bacon, fry, then drain on absorbent paper. Sprinkle over cabbage and potatoes. Serve at once. Serves 4, generously.

Kempen Ragoût

• *Stoemp Campinois* *

>   2 lbs. potatoes
>   2 lbs. carrots, sliced
>   2 large onions, diced
>   ⅛ tsp. thyme
>   1 bay leaf
>   Pepper and salt to taste
>   1½ lbs. Boston-style butt
>   2 cups beef broth *or* stock
>   2 tbsp. butter

Boil potatoes. In another pot place sliced carrots, diced onions, thyme, bay leaf, pepper and salt and Boston-style butt. Moisten with broth or stock. Cover pot and cook over a slow flame for 1½ hours. Watch it from time to time to make sure carrots do not stick to the bottom. Add water if necessary.

Remove from fire. Mash potatoes, carrots and onions together. Press this purée in a buttered ring mold; serve around the meat. Serves 4.

The purée can also be made with celery, leeks or yellow turnips.

* To serve as vegetable, omit Boston butt and substitute ham bone for flavoring.

Carrot Ragoût

• *Ragoût de Carottes*

> 2 bunches carrots
> 2 tbsp. butter
> 2 shallots *or* small onions
> 8 slices Canadian bacon
> ⅛ tsp. powdered thyme
> ¼ tsp. sugar
> 1 cup chicken broth *or* stock
> Pepper to taste
> 1 beef bouillon cube
> 1 tbsp. flour
> 1 tbsp. butter
> 1 tbsp. chopped parsley
> 1 tbsp. chopped chives

Peel and slice carrots. In a flameproof casserole melt butter, add carrots and onions, Canadian bacon, thyme and sugar. Add chicken broth and water to cover. Dust with pepper. Bring to a boil. Simmer 25 minutes.

Remove cover. Take out carrots and bacon. Keep hot. Add bouillon cube to liquid. Allow to reduce to about 1 cup over high heat. Knead flour into butter. Drop into sauce; allow to thicken and bubble for 5 minutes, stirring constantly. Add parsley and chives. Replace carrots in sauce. Bring to a boil. Dish out on pieces of toast. Serves 4.

Soused Herring or Mackerel

> 4 small herring or mackerel
> ½ cup tart white wine
> ½ cup water
> 1 tsp. whole black peppercorns
> 2 cloves
> 1 bay leaf
> 1 onion, sliced
> 3 sprigs parsley

Trim fish, cutting off heads and tails, and put in a deep, ovenproof dish with wine, water, peppercorns, cloves, bay leaf, onion and parsley. Cover and bake in a slow (300°) oven for 1 hour.

Drain fish; remove bones. Serve mackerel filets cold with mayonnaise on a bed of lettuce. Herring is more often served with Cooked Green Bean Salad (see following recipe). Serves 2.

Cooked Green Bean Salad with Mayonnaise

• *Salade du Vendredi*

> 1 No. 2 can string beans, French cut
> 1 shallot, minced
> 1 tbsp. parsley
> ⅓ cup French Dressing (see following recipe)
> ½ cup Mayonnaise (see Index)
> ½ chopped hard-cooked egg

Drain beans, add shallots and parsley, and soak 2 hours in dressing. Drain off dressing, which can be used over again. Mix with Mayonnaise and decorate with hard-cooked egg. Serves 2.

French Dressing

⅓ cup olive oil
⅓ cup corn or peanut oil
⅓ cup red wine vinegar
¼ tsp. prepared mustard
  Pepper and salt to taste

Blend all together. Makes 1 cup.

Mayonnaise

4 egg yolks
1 tsp. salt
¼ tsp. white pepper
1 tsp. dry mustard
4 tbsp. white wine vinegar
2 cups olive oil

Rinse a mixing bowl with hot water and dry thoroughly. In it place egg yolks, salt, pepper and mustard. Beat well with rotary beater or electric blender at medium speed. Add 1 teaspoon of the vinegar. Begin pouring oil, drop by drop at first, then as sauce stiffens, in a thin stream until half the oil is incorporated. Add 1 tablespoon more of the vinegar. Continue until all oil is used up. Finish with rest of vinegar. Taste and correct seasoning.

If Mayonnaise must be kept, add 1 tablespoon boiling water. Makes 2 cups.

Broiled Kippers, Flemish Style

• *Saurets à la Flamande*

> 8 kippers
> Pepper to taste

Remove backbone and large bones from kippers with a sharp kitchen knife.

Place kippers skin down under the grill. Broil five minutes under medium flame.

Dust with coarsely ground black pepper from the pepper mill. Serve with a Flemish sauce and fluffy Idaho baked potatoes.

SAUCE:

> ¼ lb. butter
> ½ cup milk
> Pepper to taste

Brown the butter in a pan. When it is a dark color and slightly burned pour the milk into the butter—very carefully, and keeping yourself at a distance from the pan.

Add pepper generously from the pepper grinder to taste.

Eel Pie

- *Anguilles en Croûte*

  2 tbsp. butter
  2 lbs. eel, skinned and cut up
  6 shallots *or* 1 small onion, diced
  2 carrots, sliced
  2 leeks, sliced
  1 bay leaf
  ⅛ tsp. thyme
  ⅛ tsp. nutmeg
  2 cloves
    Pepper and salt to taste
  ½ cup dry white wine
  2 tbsp. cornstarch
  2 egg yolks
  ½ recipe your favorite pie crust *or* ½ recipe Puff Pastry
    (see Index)

Preheat oven to 450°. Melt butter in pan; sauté pieces of eel in it until golden brown. Add shallots or onion, carrots, leeks, seasoning and wine. Bring to a boil. Reduce heat. In some of the cooking liquid, mix cornstarch and egg yolks. Stir into eel mixture and blend well. Transfer to a pie dish. Cover with unbaked, fork-pierced crust, and brush with milk. Place in a hot oven (450°), then reduce heat to 375° and bake 25 to 30 minutes. Serves 4.

Barbecued Eel

- *Anguilles sur le Gril*

>   2 lbs. large eels
>   2 eggs beaten with 2 tsp. olive oil
>   2 cups dry bread crumbs (more or less)
>   ½ cup melted butter

Have eels skinned and cut into 4-inch pieces. Dry each piece well, dip in egg-oil mixture and then in bread crumbs. Repeat. Place on charcoal broiler about 8 inches from ash-covered coals. Broil slowly and turn, brushing fish with melted butter (avoid dripping butter onto coals as any flame will char the delicate crust). Serve with

SAUCE RÉMOULADE:

Blend together:

>   1 cup Mayonnaise (see Index)
>   1 tsp. prepared mustard
>   1 tbsp. gherkins, chopped
>   ½ tbsp. capers, chopped
>   1 tsp. parsley, chopped
>   ½ tsp. tarragon & chervil, mixed and chopped
>   ¼ tsp. anchovy paste

Serves 4.

Stuffed Eels

- *Anguilles Farcies*

> 3 very big eels, skinned and cleaned (about 3 lbs. each)
> 3 cups Court-Bouillon (see Index)
> 3 hard-boiled eggs
> 1 cup mayonnaise (commercial sugarless variety accept-
> able)
> 1 tbsp. dill vinegar
> 1 tbsp. chopped parsley
> 2 cakes canned gefülte fish, mashed with a fork
> ½ tsp. dried dill *or*, preferably, 1 tsp. chopped fresh dill
> 1 2-ounce jar of caviar

Cut tail ends from eels. Simmer body part in Court-Bouillon until tender (approximately 15 minutes). Cool in liquid.

Remove bones very carefully. Split into filets. Mash hard-boiled eggs, add ½ cup mayonnaise, dill vinegar, parsley and gefülte fish. Mix thoroughly. Season to taste with dill.

Spread filling thickly between filets of eel. Top with remaining mayonnaise. Decorate with caviar and salad greens. Serves 4.

Eel Chowder

- *Anguilles des Bords de la Dyle*

3 lbs. eels
2 tbsp. butter
1 leek, white only, cut small
1 medium onion, chopped coarsely
½ cup Bière de Louvain (pale, cloudy, almost flat and very acid, but delicious on a summer day!) *or* ¼ cup beer plus ¼ cup domestic Alsatian wine
Pepper and salt to taste
½ lb. mushrooms
3 tbsp. butter
Lemon juice
1 tbsp. flour
½ cup heavy cream

Have eels cleaned, skinned and cut into 2-inch pieces. In a flameproof casserole melt butter, add leek and onion. Sauté until pale yellow. Reduce heat; simmer 5 minutes longer. Add eels and beer. Season to taste. Cover; simmer over low heat 12 to 15 minutes, or until flesh comes loose from the bones.

Meanwhile, in a small frying pan, sauté mushrooms in 2 tablespoons of the butter, sprinkle with lemon juice; season to taste. Reserve. When eels are done, carefully remove pieces from sauce with tongs or two forks. Place, with mushrooms, in a deep serving dish or earthenware casserole. Keep hot.

Incorporate flour into leftover butter with a fork, mashing it on a small dish. Drop mixture into sauce. Allow to thicken over slow heat. Add cream. Correct seasoning. Pour over the fish and mushrooms.

Serve with boiled potatoes, and drink Bière de Louvain if you have it, or the leftover Alsatian wine. Serves 4.

Chicken and Eel Matelote

- *Matelote d'Anguilles*

        6 tbsp. butter
        1 fryer chicken (3 to 4 lbs.)
       15 small onions *or* scallions
        1 can chicken broth
        2 cups claret
       ½ bay leaf
       ⅛ tsp. thyme
       ⅛ tsp. nutmeg
           Pepper to taste
        2 lbs. eels
        1 tsp. cornstarch
        8 triangular croutons (see Index)
        1 tsp chopped parsley

Melt 3 tablespoons of the butter in a deep frying pan. Over medium heat sauté pieces of chicken until golden brown on both sides. Add onion. Pour chicken broth and claret over all. Add herbs and seasonings and bring to a boil. Reduce heat; simmer 25 minutes.

Meanwhile, sauté eels in remaining butter. Add to chicken with pan drippings. Bring to a boil, reduce heat and simmer 10 minutes longer.

Remove chicken and eels from liquid. Keep hot in deep serving platter. Over high heat reduce liquid to half its volume. Dilute cornstarch in a little water and add to sauce. Allow to thicken, then pour over meats. Garnish with croutons and sprinkle with parsley. Serves 6, generously.

Braised Wild Duck

- *Canard Sauvage Braisé*

> 4 leeks, sliced
> 1 carrot, sliced
> 1 celery stalk, minced
> 1 doz. shallots *or* small onions
> 1 doz. small mushrooms, sliced
>   Pepper, salt and nutmeg to taste
> 1 whole clove
> ⅛ tsp. powdered thyme
> 1 bay leaf
> 4 sprigs parsley
> 1 cup beef consommé
> 1 jigger cognac
> 2 wild ducks, hung for 2 days

Place vegetables in casserole. Season with salt, herbs and spices. Add consommé and cognac. Place birds on top of vegetables. Cover casserole. Place in a hot oven (450°) and cook 50 minutes. Serve from casserole. Serves 4.

Quail in the Ashes

- *Cailles Sous la Cendre*

> ½ lb. mushrooms *
>   Livers from quail
> 4 quail
> 4 tbsp. butter
> 4 thin slices fat back
>   Pepper and salt to taste

* We used wild chanterelles, and placed the quail in a cooling baker's oven, wrapped in greased brown paper bags.

Chop mushrooms and livers together. Dry quail inside and out. In the cavity place mushroom and liver mixture, adding 1 tablespoon butter inside each bird. Roll them in fat back. Sprinkle with pepper and salt.

Roll birds in foil; close ends. Place packages in the hot ashes of a barbecue pit. Turn once in a while and move closer to the fire as the ashes grow colder. Cook 50 minutes. Unwrap 1 bird. Test: joints must move easily. Serves 4.

Casserole of Quail with Lettuce

- *Cailles aux Laitues*

  1/2 cup salt pork, diced
  1 cup chopped veal
  2 heads Boston lettuce
  4 quail
  6 shallots *or* 1 small onion, minced
  1 1/2 cups chicken broth
  Pepper and salt to taste

Place salt pork and chopped veal on bottom of deep casserole. Cover with lettuce leaves. On this place quail. Add shallots and chicken broth. Season. Bake uncovered in moderate (350°) oven for 45 minutes. Serves 4.

Hunter's Soup

- *Soupe Chasseur*

    1 cabbage (preferably Savoy)
    1 4-lb. fryer rabbit
   ½ lb. salt pork
  12 slices salami
    4 carrots, whole
    2 leeks, whole
    2 turnips, halved
    2 large onions
    2 whole cloves
    1 bay leaf
   ⅛ tsp. thyme
    4 sprigs parsley
     Pepper and salt to taste
    2 beef bouillon cubes

Boil whole cabbage for 5 minutes in deep water at a rolling boil. Discard the water.

Place cut up rabbit, thickly sliced salt pork, salami, carrots, leeks, turnips, onions, seasonings and bouillon cubes around cabbage in the kettle.

Add 1 quart water and simmer until all vegetables and meats are tender, or about 45 minutes. Lift vegetables and meats out of soup onto a deep serving platter. Serve soup in cups on the side with well-buttered slices of pumpernickel or German *Kommies* bread. Serves 4 to 6.

Hare or Rabbit Pâté

- *Pâté de Lièvre*

         1 large hare (*or* rabbit)
      1¾ lbs. ground pork
       ¼ tsp. thyme
       ¼ tsp. nutmeg
         1 bay leaf
            Pepper and salt with heavy hand
       ½ cup cognac
         1 lb. raw ham, sliced and cut in wide strips
         1 lb. fat back, sliced

Have butcher skin, clean and remove bones from a large hare. Cut tender part of back into filets and reserve. Put the rest of the hare meat, including giblets and liver, through grinder. Mix with ground pork. Add seasonings and ¼ cup of the cognac. Let stand for 1 hour.

Meanwhile, have sliced ham and hare filets in a bowl. Season and cover with remaining cognac. Let stand for 1 hour.

Line a porcelain or earthenware casserole with strips of fat back. Fill with 1 inch of meat mixture. Then put a layer of ham strips, filet strips, and repeat procedure until casserole is full, topping with fat back, which should cover entire surface of last layer.

Cover casserole. Place it in a shallow pan with water and bake in moderate over (350°) for 1 hour and 15 minutes. Serve cold. Yields 12 slices.

For a first course or buffet. Keeps very well in a cool place as long as top layer of fat is undisturbed.

Poacher's Stew

- *Pot-au-Feu du Braconnier*

    1 hare *or* rabbit, past its tender age
    1 partridge *or* game cock, past its tender age
    6 cloves garlic
    ½ lb. salt pork
    3 celery stalks
    2 celeriacs
       Pepper and salt to taste
    ⅛ tsp. powdered thyme
    ½ bay leaf
    4 sprigs parsley
    4 tbsp. butter

Place game and bird in a 6-quart pot. Cover with 3 quarts water. Bring to a boil. Skim carefully. Reduce heat and add garlic and salt pork. Cook 2 hours, then add celeries and seasonings. Simmer until vegetables are done. Remove vegetables and purée them, while meat continues to cook. Place puréed vegetables in a casserole, add butter and correct the seasoning. Keep warm over very low heat until meat is done. Cut up game and bird. Place pieces on top of purée.

Serve with thin pumpernickel bread sandwiches and a cup of strained liquid on the side. Serves 6, generously.

Rabbit Stew with Egg Sauce

- *Lapin à la Poulette*

      3 tbsp. butter
      1 fryer rabbit (2 to 3 lbs.) cut in pieces
      1 cup dry white wine
      2 carrots, sliced
      6 shallots *or* 1 small onion, sliced
     12 small mushrooms, whole
      1 bay leaf
     ⅛ tsp. powdered thyme
     ⅛ tsp. powdered oregano
      1 clove
     ⅛ tsp. grated nutmeg
        Pepper and salt to taste
      4 egg yolks diluted with 2 tbsp. light cream
     ½ tbsp. lemon juice

Melt butter in skillet. In it sauté pieces of rabbit until lightly browned. Cover with wine and 1 cup water. Add vegetables, herbs and seasonings. Bring to a boil. Cover. Reduce heat and simmer 45 minutes or until tender. Remove meat and vegetables from liquid in skillet.

To make sauce remove liquid from heat. Add egg yolk mixture, stirring constantly. Add lemon juice. Taste, correct seasoning. Replace on heat and bring just below boiling point (DO NOT BOIL). Pour over meat in serving dish. Serve with Cabbage and Potato Casserole (see Index). Serves 4.

Roast Jack Rabbit

- *Lapin de Garenne Rôti*

        1 rabbit, 7 to 8 lbs.
        2 tbsp. prepared mustard
        4 slices bacon
            Pepper and salt to taste
        3 tbsp. butter
        1 pt. heavy cream (more or less)
        1 tbsp. cognac (optional)

Preheat oven to 375°. Discard head, front legs and breast of rabbit. Reserve for other use. Rub saddle and back legs with mustard. Cover back and legs with bacon. Season. Place in an open roasting pan with butter. When well browned on top (about 45 minutes) baste with 3 tablespoons of the heavy cream. Repeat every 10 minutes until rabbit is done (about 1½ hours).

Place rabbit on hot platter. Keep hot. Deglaze roasting pan over high heat by adding ¼ cup water and scraping sides and bottom of pan. Stir well. Add leftover cream and cognac if desired. Taste and correct seasoning. Pour some of the sauce over rabbit. Serve the rest in a sauceboat. Surround rabbit with applesauce, water cress, French fried potatoes and sautéed chanterelles or commercial mushrooms. Serves 4 to 6.

Pork Stew

• *Ragoût de Porc*

>   2 tbsp. butter
>   1 large Spanish onion, minced
>   2½ lbs. shoulder of pork, cut up
>   ½ tsp. celery salt
>   Salt to taste
>   2 cloves
>   6 peppercorns, crushed
>   2 cups canned consommé *or* stock
>   1 cup shredded red cabbage
>   ½ apple, diced
>   ¾ cup heavy cream

Melt butter in a flameproof casserole. Add minced onion and pork. Over medium heat, brown meat slowly on all sides. Add seasoning, consommé, cabbage and apple. Bring to boiling point. Reduce heat and simmer 2 hours, covered.

Remove cover, increase heat and reduce liquid by half by boiling. Add cream. Taste and correct seasoning. Serve with boiled or mashed potatoes. Serves 4.

Beef Stew

- *Hutsepot*

    2 lbs. lean beef for stewing
    1 lb. lean lamb for stewing
      Pepper and salt to taste
    4 carrots
    4 celery stalks, halved
    4 turnips, quartered
    4 onions
    4 leeks
    2 parsnips, halved
    1 cup green peas, cooked or canned
    1 cup string beans, cooked or canned
    2 tbsp. cornstarch
    2 egg yolks

Place meats in flameproof casserole. Cover with water, season. Bring to a boil. Reduce heat and simmer for 1½ hours. Add all vegetables except cooked peas and beans and more boiling water to cover. Bring again to a boil. Reduce heat and cook vegetables until tender. Take out 1 cup liquid. Cool it.

Add beans and peas to the pot. Dilute cornstarch and egg yolks in cooled cup of liquid. Stir into stew and allow to thicken by bringing to boiling point. Remove from heat. Serves 4 portions from the pot. The same dish is often made with pork and beef. In this case add 1 cabbage, quartered.

Veal Birds

• *Vogels Zonder Kop*

4 thin slices beef
¼ lb. ground veal
¼ lb. ground pork
1 slice bread dipped in milk
  Salt, pepper, chopped parsley
2 tbsp. butter (more or less)
½ tsp. dill, chopped
1 tbsp. butter mixed with 1 tsp. cornstarch
1 tbsp. cream

MARINATING LIQUID:

½ cup dill vinegar
1 tbsp. oil
1½ cups water
  Thyme, bay leaf, onion

Marinate beef for 2 hours. Make a stuffing of the veal, pork, bread, salt, pepper and chopped parsley.

Remove beef from marinating liquid. Spread with chopped meat mixture; roll and tie with string. Brown in butter on all sides, add 1 tablespoon of the marinating liquid, cover and simmer 20-25 minutes.

Before serving remove fat from pan drippings and deglaze pan by adding ½ cup boiling water and scraping down sides. Add chopped dill and thicken with butter-cornstarch mixture; remove from heat and finish with cream.

Correct seasoning. Cut the strings from the rolls of beef and serve. Serves 4.

Smothered Steak

- *Estouffade Chevaline*

      4 tbsp. butter
      5 medium onions, sliced
      1 carrot, sliced
      5 celery stalks, sliced
      2 leeks, sliced
      1 bay leaf
    ⅛ tsp. powdered or fresh thyme
    ½ clove garlic, crushed
      3 tbsp. bottled Escoffier Sauce Diable
         Pepper and salt to taste
    ¼ cup claret or light beer
      4 individual horsemeat steaks *or* flank steaks (beef, if
         preferred)
    ½ cup flour
      4 slices whole wheat bread

Melt 2 tablespoons of the butter in flameproof casserole; lightly brown onions in it. Add carrots, celery, leeks, bay leaf, thyme, garlic, Sauce Diable and pepper and salt to taste. Moisten with ¾ cup water and claret or beer.

Melt remaining butter in a skillet. Sauté steaks until brown on both sides. Season. Add steaks and pan drippings to vegetables in casserole. Cover. On pastry board mix flour with enough water to make a dough. Seal cover with strips of dough. Cook 2 hours over very low heat or in oven at 300°. Break seal. Serve from casserole over thick slices of buttered whole wheat bread. Serves 4.

White Sausage

- *Boudin Blanc*

    1 lb. lean pork meat
    1 lb. bacon
    3 eggs
    ½ cup finely chopped onions
    ⅛ tsp. pepper
      Salt to taste
    ½ tsp. marjoram
    3 slices white bread dipped in milk
      Nutmeg
      Pork casings

Put lean pork meat and bacon through grinder. Place in a bowl; add eggs, chopped onions, pepper, salt, marjoram, bread and nutmeg. Mix together.

Stuff this mixture in pork casings, carefully washed. Fill only ¾ full. Tie up sausages in 8-inch links, so that they may be handled easily without breaking. While filling the sausages the skin must be pierced with large pin to let out air.

Place links on a grill or wicker rack and lower into a casserole ¾ full of boiling water. Keep water just above boiling point. Poach for 20 minutes. Do not cover while cooking as sausages might burst. Chill. May be served hot or cold.

Grilled White Sausage

Roll sausage in foil. Broil under a low flame or over the ashes of a barbecue pit. Serve with a purée of potatoes and applesauce or fried apples.

Sausage Skimmings

• *Kruip-Uit*

> ¼ lb. sausage skimmings
> ¼ lb. ground pork
> 1 bay leaf
> ⅛ tsp. thyme
> Pepper and salt to taste
> 3 slices fat back

When sausages break accidentally in the making, skim the water in the pot for any sausage meat. Mix these skimmings with pork and seasoning. Line a coffee can or small mold with fat back. Place meats in it. Cover with the lid or aluminum foil. Place in a pan with water and bake for 1½ hours in medium (350°) oven. Makes ½ pound loaf.

Slice and serve cold with buttered rye bread.

Sour Cherries in Vinegar

• *Kriekskens*

> 4 lbs. sour cherries
> 2 cups granulated sugar
> ½ tsp. allspice
> ½ tsp. cinnamon
> ¼ tsp. powdered cloves
> 2 cups cider vinegar (more or less)
> Peel of 1 lemon

Remove stems from washed cherries. In earthen crock or wide-mouth glass apothecary jar, place a layer of cherries, sprinkle with sugar and spices. Repeat until crock is nearly filled.

Boil vinegar and lemon peel together for 3 minutes. When cold, pour over cherries. Tape cover of crock or jar. Store until winter. Serve with cold veal or chicken. Yield: about 2 quarts.

Pears Stewed in Coffee

- *Compote de Poires*

    8 large pears, with stems
    1 cup weak coffee
    1 cup Vanilla Sugar (see following recipe)
    1 bay leaf
    2 cloves

Peel pears, leaving them whole. In a pot bring coffee to a boil with 1½ cups water. Add sugar and spices. Reduce heat. Poach pears in liquid until tender all the way through.

Remove pears. Thicken juice by boiling over high heat until reduced to half the volume. Pour over the pears; chill. Serve cold. Serves 4.

Vanilla Sugar

- *Sucre Vanillé*

Buy 2 vanilla beans at a specialty food shop. Place them in a canister with 1 pound granulated sugar. Cover and allow to remain untouched for a week. From time to time replenish sugar; add 1 vanilla bean every 6 months.

This gives a much finer flavor than vanilla extract and can be used wherever extract is called for. One tablespoon Vanilla Sugar equals ¼ teaspoon extract. Decrease amount of sugar in recipe accordingly.

Seckel Pears Sweet-Sour

- *Bergamottes à l'Aigre-Doux*

> 5 cups granulated sugar
> 1 qt. cider vinegar
> Peel of 1 lemon
> 1 cinnamon stick
> ¼ tsp. powdered mace *or* nutmeg
> ¼ tsp. salt
> 8 lbs. small Seckel pears, peeled whole and with stems

Melt sugar in vinegar. Add lemon peel, spices and salt. Place pears in a pot and pour vinegar-sugar mixture over them. Bring to a boil. Simmer 2 hours, uncovered.

Pack pears in sterile glass jars. Pour syrup over them. Seal. Will keep indefinitely. Yield: 6 quarts.

Serve as accompaniment to cold poultry or white meats.

Peach Marmalade

- *Marmalade de Pêches*

> 5 lbs. small white peaches
> 3 lbs. granulated sugar

Stone and quarter peaches. Place them, unskinned, in a deep pot and cover with sugar. Start on slow heat until the sugar is melted.

In the meantime crush 10 peach pits. Remove the bitter almonds. Dip them in boiling water, remove skins. Sliver on a grate or with a knife and add to marmalade. Bring fruit to a rolling boil; skim and reduce heat a little. Stir constantly and keep boiling for 20 minutes.

Test a teaspoonful. Cool, place between forefinger and thumb, separate fingers a little. Thread should form when marmalade is done. Skim again. Pack into sterile glasses and seal with paraffin. Yield: 8 6-ounce jars.

Sour Cherry Marmalade

• *Kriekskens*

> 5 lbs. sour cherries
> 5 lbs. granulated sugar

Stem and pit washed cherries. Tie pits in a cloth. Place cherries and pits in a deep pot with ¼ cup water. Cover with sugar. Start cooking over slow heat until sugar is melted. Bring to a rolling boil over high heat. Skim carefully. Reduce heat slightly and continue to boil, stirring constantly for 15 minutes.

Test a teaspoonful. Cool, place between thumb and forefinger, separate fingers a little. Thread should form when marmalade is done.

Skim again. Pour into sterile jars and seal with paraffin. Makes 12 6-ounce jars.

Sand Torte Pastry

• *Pâte Sablée*

> ¼ lb. butter
> 1½ cup flour
> 1 tsp. baking powder
> ¼ cup Vanilla Sugar (see Index)
> 2 egg yolks

Mix all ingredients together, using fingers, until dough feels like modeling clay. Pat onto bottom and 2 inches up the sides of a 10-inch spring form pan.

Fill and bake according to recipe or, to make a shell, bake it 30 minutes at 375°.

Cherry Torte

- *Tarte aux Cerises*

     2½ lbs. sour cherries *
      1 cup sugar
      1 recipe Sand Torte Pastry (see preceding recipe)
     ¼ cup confectioners' (powdered) sugar

Remove pits and stems from cherries. Tie ½ cup of pits in a small cloth and place in pot with cherries. Add sugar and 4 tablespoons water. Bring to a boil, reduce heat and simmer 3 minutes. Remove from heat. Cool. Discard pits. Drain cherries thoroughly. (Juice is excellent when used in gelatin desserts.)

Place drained cherries in unbaked Sand Torte Pastry. Bake 35 minutes in quick moderate oven (375°), 4 inches from bottom of oven. Cherries will look shriveled. Remove outer rim from spring mold. Cool torte. Loosen carefully from bottom of form. Slide very gently onto cake platter.

Just before serving dust heavily with confectioners' sugar. Serves 6.

* 2 No. 2 cans of sour pitted cherries may be substituted for fresh cherries. Omit sugar. Drain cherries and put directly into pastry shell.

Doughball Torte

- *Knibbekes Tarte*

  ½ recipe Pâte Brisée (see Index)
  ¼ lb. butter
  1⅔ cups granulated sugar
  1 cup sifted flour
  2 tbsp. melted butter
  2 tbsp. brown sugar

Line well-greased 9-inch pie plate with rolled out Pâte Brisée. Make fluted edging. In a bowl cream butter and sugar, gradually adding flour. When dough is ready to handle turn it onto lightly floured board. Shape into a loaf. Cover and let stand 1 hour in a cool place.

Divide and shape it into little balls the size of a walnut. Place these little balls, one next to the other, on pastry in the pie plate. Pour melted butter over them. Sprinkle with brown sugar.

Bake in moderate oven (350°) for 45 minutes. When done, allow to remain a few minutes in the pan, until pie shrinks away from it. Then, with a spatula carefully loosen torte at one side and, holding pie dish tipped, turn it to let the air in all around the torte. Slide onto wire rack and cool. Serves 6.

Freezes well. Thaw out at room temperature. Reheat in slow oven for a few minutes before serving.

Tournai, Mons and The Borinage

Where Tournai now stands, Julius Caesar and his legionnaires once laid waste a burgh. One hundred years later it was rebuilt to become the earliest seat of Gallic royalty. Later the town became famous for the gold cloth manufactured there by special order of the Merovingian kings. In 1633 under the nave of Tournai's magnificent, five-steepled Romanesque cathedral were discovered 300 golden bees nearly 1,000 years old. These were the bees Napoleon Bonaparte was to use on his coronation mantle as a symbolic means of linking his concept of a French empire with the earliest kingdoms of Gaul.

Until 100 years ago the Borinage had remained a pastoral province. Today it is a densely populated industrial center. Yet in this area the Belgian coal digger still keeps his love of the land. Outside the city limits he rents a few feet of garden, which he fences in with chicken wire. There he grows peas, parsley, lettuce, tomatoes, and for the winter, celeriac, leeks and Brussels sprouts.

Although the people of the Borinage are proud of their slag heaps, coal mines, glass works, blast furnaces, rolling mills, wire mills, pottery works—their deepest sense of pleasure is derived from participation in regional celebrations. Among the oldest in Europe, these festivals are rooted in traditions so ancient that they are a continued source of interest to folklorists.

At Ecaussines, on the first Monday after Pentecost, marriageable boys and girls as well as spinsters and bachelors gather from all the provinces for a gigantic party, the *goûter matrimonial,* a feast of fruit pies and rice torten, held under the walls of an ancient and forbidding castle. The invitation to the party may come in the form of a little sand path, a *sentier d'amour,* which the secret lover traces from his house to that of his beloved at dawn on the first of May.

Like Wales, Borinage is a singing country. The miners of Frameries, Paturages and other small towns have, under the aegis of St. Cecilia, founded five choral societies and produced some of the leading singers of the Belgian stage. When festival time comes around choral singers naturally participate.

Thus, on Trinity Sunday after High Mass, in the market square of Mons and the street leading to the ruins of the Count of Hainaut's ancient castle, the legend of a local St. George is re-enacted. In front of a multitude of singers, bands, mummers and onlookers shouting and cheering *"V'la l'Doudou, V'la Lumeçon!"* Gilles de Chin rides again, to defeat the monster with the aid of his "wild men." There may be some truth to the legend, for in the natural history museum in Brussels are the prehistoric remains of a colony of iguanodons—one of the largest of the dinosaurs—found in a quarry at Bernissart, a few miles away from Tournai. Gilles de Chin could not possibly have slain this prehistoric beast, but a more modest skull of a huge lizard is claimed as his trophy, and the *Chin-chins,* or leaf-clad "wild men," who are his supporting cast in this play may be, so say folklorists, a survival of a much more ancient ritual. Other traces of this ritual, vaguely Christianized, are found all over the Walloon or French-speaking part of Belgium.

A great deal of speculation has been aroused among scientists by the Feast of Alion, which is generally explained as a survival of the rites of Helios, or spring. It is a feast of young people: dressed in fancy robes, covered with garlands of spring flowers and their arms entwined in a pretty gesture, a young couple is chosen to stand on a trestle table or under a trellised bower while their neighbors dance around them. A folk singer, sometimes accompanied by a fife and a drum, chants one of the oldest pentatonic songs on the continent. It is a song too ancient to be understood by the participants; the words are now taught by rote, year after year. Chicken and lamb and sometimes roast kid are served traditionally on that day.

Another curious spring festival is held at Grammont. The burgomaster, aldermen, the city councilmen, the firemen, the *curé* and people from miles around follow to the top of a hill thirty men bearing huge baskets of specially baked cakes called *craquelins.* On the Oudenberg (old mountain) stands a platform, upon which is a table set with wine, a beautiful antique silver cup and a bowl of small live fish. Every important person in town is called upon to swallow a live fish with a mouthful of wine. Those who have drunk the fish then toss the cakes to the scrambling populace. There are never enough to go around, and of course the cakes bring good luck to those who catch them.

The most spectacular festival of Hainaut is the Mardi Gras at Binche. It seems to have originated shortly after the conquest of Mexico by the Spaniards, at a time when the Hapsburgs of Spain were overlords of Belgium. The costumes created for the visit of some Spanish grandee have been passed on as heirlooms and are displayed in yearly celebrations ever since. To be a "Gilles" in Binche—that is, to own one of these costly costumes, to participate in this three-day frenzied parade, to dance as the Indians did in an asymmetric rhythm entirely foreign to these parts, to pelt neighbors with Seville oranges—has become the ambition of every boy and man in town.

I have watched from a balcony overlooking the *Grand' Place* the movements of the crowd, the rhythmical bobbing of the Gilles' five-foot ostrich-feathered headgear tracing the undulating pattern of their dances. Always, somewhat in the rear of the room where we sat, a cold supper was laid out for visitors: *raviers* of colorful cooked salads, platters of sweet water fish *en daube,* a *chaud-froid* of capon *carolorégienne* with its *garniture* of truffles, *quenelles,* mushroom caps, and sweetbreads; roast pork *à l'escavèche,* glass jars of brandied grapes, mounds of macaroons, and *dorées,* the golden saffron-flavored rice torten.

In the flickering candlelight the decanters of Burgundy wine imported from France made ruby patterns on the damask cloth and always when new guests wandered in the hostess asked: *"Vous prendrez bien quelque chose avec nous?"* The polite retort never failed: *"Avec plaisir."*

For it is the accepted custom anywhere in Belgium to share some food or drink with your hosts. To refuse what is offered is to deny the mistress of the house the privilege of proving the truth of Julius Caesar's words: "The Belgians are the most hospitable of all Gauls."

Pea Soup

• *Soupe aux Pois*

  1 smoked pork butt *or* ½ smoked pork tenderloin
  1 lb. split peas
  1 tsp. garlic salt
 ½ bay leaf
 ⅛ tsp. dried thyme
  3 peppercorns, bruised
 ½ tsp. celery seed
  1 tbsp. butter
  1 small onion, minced
  1 cup cubed croutons (see Index)

In a soup pot cover the meat with 3 quarts water. Add peas and seasonings and bring to a boil. Reduce heat and simmer 2 hours. Taste and correct seasoning.

When soup is nearly done melt butter in a small pan and brown onion slowly and lightly. Remove meat from soup and cut into bite-sized pieces. Pour soup into tureen. Add browned onion, meat and Croutons. Serves 6, generously.

Green salad and cheese make this into a complete meal.

Red Cabbage Soup

• *Soupe au Chou Rouge*

> 1 medium-sized red cabbage
> 3 medium onions, sliced
> 1 tart apple, diced
> 3 large potatoes, diced
> ½ stick butter
> 1 can beef consommé
> ⅛ tsp. thyme
> ⅛ tsp. garlic salt
> ½ bay leaf
>   Ham, steak or veal bone
>   Pepper and salt to taste
>   Croutons (see Index)

Shred cabbage, discarding large ribs and core. Boil for 15 minutes in salt water. Drain.

In soup kettle simmer onions in butter until golden. Add all other ingredients, except croutons. Cover with consommé and 2 quarts of water and allow to cook slowly for 2 hours. Blend in electric blender or force through sieve or food mill. Serve hot with croutons. Yield: 8 cups.

The prettiest purple soup you ever saw!

Pumpkin Soup

- *Soupe au Potiron*

        2 cups pumpkin meat, canned
        1 onion
        1 bay leaf
        4 cloves
        4 cups chicken broth
            Pepper and salt to taste
        1 cup heavy cream *or* 1 can evaporated milk
        1 tsp. Worcestershire Sauce
        1 tbsp. parsley, finely chopped

Simmer pumpkin meat, onions, bay leaf, cloves in chicken broth for ½ hour. Season to taste. Rub through a sieve. Add heavy cream and Worcestershire Sauce. Mix well. Top each plate or cup with chopped parsley. Yield: about 5 cups.

Leek Salad

- *Salade de Poireaux*

Prepare 1 day ahead

        12 leeks
         1 tsp. peppercorns
         1 tsp. chopped onion
         1 tsp. chopped parsley
         ¾ cup French Dressing (see Index)

Cut off green tops and roots of leeks. Spread leaves of white part slightly and wash clean of all dirt. Slice into 2-inch pieces. Boil in salted water for 10 minutes, uncovered. Drain. Place in a salad bowl with peppercorns, onion and parsley. Add French Dressing, toss and allow to stand overnight. Toss, taste and correct seasoning.

No other garnish is added to this hors d'oeuvre, but it is often served with sliced frankfurters in a Rémoulade Sauce (see Index) or with sliced salami. Serves 4 to 6.

Beet Salad

• *Salade de Betteraves*

Prepare 1 day ahead

> 1 No. 2 can sliced beets
> 2 cloves garlic, crushed
> 1 tsp. chopped onion
> 1 tsp. chopped parsley
> ½ cup French Dressing (see Index) OMITTING mustard

Drain beets. Place in a bowl with all ingredients and allow to stand overnight. Toss; correct seasoning to taste. Serves 4 as an hors d'oeuvre. May also be added to lettuce for a winter salad.

Kidney Bean Salad

• *Salade d'Haricots*

Prepare 1 day ahead

> 1 No. 2 can red kidney beans
> 1 tsp. chopped onion
> 1 tsp. chopped parsley
> ¼ tsp. oregano
> ½ cup French Dressing (see Index) OMITTING mustard

Drain beans. Place in a bowl with all ingredients and allow to stand overnight. Toss, correct seasoning to taste. Serves 4 as an hors d'oeuvre.

Coalminer's Omelet

• *Omelette du Charbonnier*

> 1 cup leftover veal or beef stew with gravy *or* 1 cup sautéed sausage meat
> 2 cups cooked potatoes, diced
> ½ cup salt pork, cubed
> 9 eggs
> 2 tbsp. iced water
> Pepper and salt to taste
> 6 tbsp. butter

With a fork, shred and mash cold leftover stew meat with some of the gravy. Reserve. In a frying pan brown potatoes and salt pork. Reserve, keeping hot.

Break eggs into a bowl. Add iced water, pepper and salt. Beat lightly with a fork until well mixed. Add half the butter in dots; it will melt while eggs are cooking.

Heat heavy iron pan. Melt remaining butter. When it sizzles pour in beaten eggs and reduce heat to medium. With a fork slowly bring the edges of the omelet toward the center in order to give it height. Tilt pan to make liquid run toward edges.

Omelet is done when there remains only a thin uncooked film on the surface of the omelet. Place meat in center. Arrange potatoes in a ring around the edges. Do not fold. Slide onto a platter. Serves 6.

Egg and Potato Casserole

- *Oeufs à la Tomate*

        6 hard-cooked eggs
        2 tbsp. butter
        ¼ cup soft bread crumbs
        2 tbsp. milk
        1 tsp. dried chervil *or* chopped parsley
          Pepper and salt to taste
        3 tbsp. canned tomato purée
        4 cups mashed potatoes
          Dusting of paprika

Cut eggs in half lengthwise while still hot. Remove yolks and mash, with a fork, together with butter, bread crumbs, milk and seasonings. Heap yolk mixture into whites.

Blend tomato purée with mashed potatoes and line a shallow buttered casserole or baking dish with this mixture. Push stuffed eggs into purée-potato mixture and dust with paprika. Bake in slow oven (250°) 20 minutes. Serves 4.

Egg and Onion Casserole

- *Oeufs à l'Oignon*

        2 tbsp. butter
        2 large onions, sliced very thin
        2 tbsp. flour
        1 cup stock *or* canned chicken broth
          Pepper, salt, nutmeg to taste
        1 tbsp. heavy cream
        1 tsp. lemon juice
        6 hard-cooked eggs, quartered lengthwise

Melt butter in skillet, add onion slices and simmer over low heat until tender without allowing to brown. Add flour, stirring vigorously. Increase heat and allow to brown lightly; then add stock or broth, a little at a time, stirring continuously while sauce bubbles and thickens. When all the broth is added continue to cook for 5 minutes, stirring all the while. Season to taste with pepper, salt and nutmeg. Add heavy cream, lemon juice and eggs.

Place in a shallow casserole. Bake 10 minutes in moderate oven (350°). Serve with Smothered Potatoes (see Index). Serves 4.

Eggs en Cocotte

- *Oeufs en Cocotte*

3 tbsp. butter
8 whole eggs
2 egg whites
　Pepper and salt to taste
8 strips bacon, fried and crumbled
3 tbsp. chopped parsley
1 cup sautéed mushrooms
3 tbsp. heavy cream

Select a flameproof casserole, 4 x 4 x 2 or 6 x 2 x 2, with a cover. In it, melt butter and bring to sizzling point. Break eggs into butter and add extra whites. Season. Cover and cook over very slow heat for 20 minutes without disturbing. Yolks should remain soft and be covered with a whitish film. Sprinkle bacon crumbs, parsley and mushrooms over top. Add heavy cream. Serves 4.

Macaroni au Gratin

• *Macaroni au Gratin*

½ package (8 ozs.) elbow macaroni
⅓ lb. freshly grated Gruyère cheese
2 cups Béchamel Sauce (see Index)
1 lb. ham, chopped by hand
1 tomato, sliced
½ lb. sliced, sautéed mushrooms
   Bread crumbs, butter

Place macaroni in boiling salted water and cook uncovered for 20 minutes. Drain in colander and rinse quickly under a stream of cold water.

Melt cheese in hot Béchamel Sauce and add, with cooked ham, to macaroni. Pour ⅓ of this mixture into a casserole. Cover with a layer of sliced tomato and mushrooms. Top with macaroni mixture, then repeat tomato and mushrooms and finish with remaining ⅓ of macaroni. Sprinkle with bread crumbs and garnish with small dabs of butter.

Broil until golden brown. Serve hot. Serves 4.

This dish may be prepared ahead of time, kept warm in a 250° oven and browned at the last minute.

Chicken with Bacon and Noodles

• *Poule aux Nouilles*

> 1 stewing chicken (5 to 6 lbs.)
> 1 celery stalk
> 1 carrot
> 1 onion
> 5 sprigs parsley
> ½ bay leaf
> 2 cloves
> Pepper and salt to taste
> 6 slices bacon
> 1 carrot, sliced
> 1 onion, sliced
> ¾ lb. wide noodles

In a pot place chicken, celery stalk, carrot, onion, parsley and seasonings. Cover with water; bring to a boil. Reduce heat and poach 1 hour. Remove chicken from broth.

Line a flameproof casserole with bacon, add carrot and onion and place chicken on top of vegetables and bacon. Moisten with 1 cup of the broth. Cover and simmer ½ hour or until tender.

Meanwhile strain remaining broth, bring to a boil and cook noodles in it, uncovered. Drain noodles and reserve liquid for stock pot. Place noodles in a heap on serving platter and keep hot while carving chicken. Place chicken on top of noodles and garnish with bacon and vegetables. Serves 4 to 6.

Tongue Soufflé

- *Soufflé au Vin de Madère*

      1 lb. macaroni
    1½ cups Béchamel Sauce (see Index)
      ½ cup slivered Switzerland Swiss cheese
      1 cup ground leftover tongue
      ½ cup Madeira or sherry wine
      1 tbsp. tomato purée
      4 egg yolks
      4 egg whites, beaten stiff
      ½ lb. sliced tongue or prosciutto
        Pepper and salt to taste

Place macaroni in boiling salted water and cook 20 minutes, uncovered. Drain-in strainer and rinse quickly under a stream of cold water.

Butter a 1-quart pudding mold on all sides. Line mold with macaroni, placing strand against strand, leaving no openings. (Deep Pyrex bowl, with double cover of foil securely fastened, is good substitute.)

In a bowl, mix ¾ of the Béchamel, slivered cheese, ground tongue, tomato purée, half of the wine and 3 of the egg yolks. Fold in beaten egg whites. Pour mixture into macaroni-lined mold to two inches below top. Cover mold securely and steam 2 hours in any large pot with a cover, on top of stove or in oven, making sure bubbling water stays below cover line.

Warm sliced tongue in double boiler. Arrange the slices around edge of a round platter and unmold soufflé in center. Rush to table. Serve with a separate sauce made by combining remaining Béchamel, wine and egg yolk, seasoned to taste. Serves 6.

Mock Turtle Stew

- *Tête de Veau en Tortue*

        1 head of veal, ready to cook
        1 extra veal tongue
        1 onion
        2 sprigs parsley
      1/8 tsp. thyme
        1 bay leaf
          Pepper and salt to taste
        1 lb. small mushrooms
        1 tsp. butter
        1 cup stock
        1 cup Madeira wine
        1 cup Béchamel Sauce (see Index)
        1 can tomato purée
      1/2 cup gherkins, sliced
        5 pimiento-stuffed olives, thinly sliced
        4 hard-cooked eggs, quartered
        6 croutons (see Index)

In a large pot bring meats to a boil. Pour off water, then cook meats 1½ hours with onion and seasonings in just enough water to cover. Remove meat from bones and cut in 2-inch cubes. Peel the tongue and cut into thin slices.

Sauté mushrooms in butter at the bottom of pot large enough to hold all the meat. Add meats, stock, Madeira, Béchamel, and tomato purée. Simmer all together 15 minutes, stirring often. Taste, correct seasoning. To serve, place meats in a deep platter. Garnish around edges with gherkins, olives, hard-cooked eggs and croutons. Serves 6.

COLD LEFTOVER STEW, IN ASPIC: *

Over a bowl of ice, with pastry brush spread a coating of liquid canned consommé Madrilène over the sides of a mold. Garnish in pretty designs with sliced black and green olives and sliced egg; and allow to set. Pour in the cool stew and allow to set for several hours. Turn out on a bed of lettuce. Serves 6.

Smothered Calf's Liver

• *Fois de Veau à l'Étouffée*

>   3 tbsp. butter
>   1 whole calf's liver
>   1 cup diced salt pork
>   ¼ cup minced onion
>   ⅛ tsp. dried thyme
>   ½ bay leaf
>   1 piece dried orange peel (size of a silver dollar)
>   Pepper and salt to taste
>   ¾ cup red Burgundy wine
>   ⅔ cup beef broth *or* stock
>   1 tsp. cornstarch diluted in ¼ cup beef broth *or* stock

In a flameproof casserole heat butter to sizzling point. Place in it liver, salt pork, onion and seasonings. Add wine and broth or stock. Bring to a boil. Cover tightly and twist a towel around rim of the casserole. Reduce heat to medium and simmer for 2½ hours or until tender. Remove liver from casserole, slice it and keep warm on a heated platter.

* Fine gourmets make this dish sumptuous by garnishing it with crayfish, *quenelles,* sweetbreads, truffles cooked in cognac. Lazy cooks can buy it ready-made in portions at the Belgian delicatessen.

Strain juices. Bring to a boil. Add diluted cornstarch, stirring rapidly until thickened. Pour over the meat. Serves 4 to 6.

Casserole of Veal or Oxtails Paysanne

- *Queues de Veau*

      1 head of cabbage (about 2 lbs.)
      2 cups beef consommé
      1 onion, sliced
      1 carrot, sliced
     ½ bay leaf
     ⅛ tsp. thyme
      3 sprigs parsley
        Pepper and salt to taste
      6 veal *or* 2 oxtails
      2 tbsp. butter
      1 tbsp. flour
     ½ lb. bacon, sliced
     ½ cup heavy cream

Quarter cabbage, removing hard ribs and core. Place in casserole, spreading leaves. Cover with consommé. Add vegetables and herbs. Place tails in center. Blend butter and flour with a fork. Add to liquid in casserole. Simmer, covered, for 1 hour in a medium hot (375°) oven. Taste and correct seasoning.

Fry bacon, drain on absorbent paper and crumble to bits.

Just before serving add cream and shake casserole to mix it with sauce. Sprinkle bacon on top. Serves 6.

Braised Beef Tongue

· *Langue de Boeuf Braisée*

    1 smoked beef tongue
    6 carrots, quartered lengthwise
   10 shallots
    3 medium onions, sliced
    4 celery stalks
    4 leeks (optional) *or* endive stalks
   ⅛ tsp. powdered thyme
   ½ bay leaf
    1 clove garlic, crushed
   ½ cup white wine
    4 tbsp. butter
   ½ cup Madeira *or* port wine
    8 small boiled potatoes *or* 1 can Irish potatoes, drained

Boil tongue and carrots for ½ hour in a large pot in plenty of water. Discard the water. Peel tongue. In a deep pan place tongue with vegetables and seasonings, 1 cup water and white wine. Cover, bring to a boil, reduce heat and simmer for 1 hour.* Remove cover. Add butter. Continue cooking, allowing all water to evaporate and meat and vegetables to brown on high heat. Add Madeira wine. Taste and correct seasoning. Add potatoes. Serves 6.

* May be cooked 1 hour in preheated oven (350°) if preferred. Then back on top of stove.

Head Cheese

• *Fromage de Porc*

> 1 pig's head
> 1 bay leaf
> ½ tsp. peppercorns
> 1 tsp. celery seed
>   Salt and pepper to taste

Have the butcher remove the eyes and brains from the head. Soak head for a few minutes in lukewarm water. Brush it well with a wire brush.

Place in pot with bay leaf, peppercorns and celery seed. Cover with cold water and bring to a boil. Skim and cook until tender and meat leaves the bones.

Remove meat. Cut into small pieces, including the ears. Skin the tongue and chop it up. Mix well together with salt and pepper to taste and add one ladle of cooking stock. Pack into bowl, place a weight on top and allow to set overnight.

Serve cold. Slice for sandwiches. Yield: 1½ to 2-pound loaf.

Head Cheese Aspic

- *Kip-Kap*

    4 pigs' feet
    3 lbs. beef shank
    1 onion
    5 sprigs parsley
    ½ cup herb-flavored wine vinegar
    ⅛ tsp. thyme
    1 bay leaf
    ⅛ tsp. cayenne pepper
    4 cloves
    ⅛ tsp. black pepper
    ⅛ tsp. nutmeg
        Pepper and salt to taste

Cook feet and beef shank with onion and parsley in 2 quarts salted water. Reserve broth.

Remove meat and allow to cool. Then remove bones from feet and shank and mince coarsely. Place the meats in a large pot with four ladles of juice, vinegar, herbs and seasonings.

Bring to a boil. Rinse a mold or Pyrex bowl with cold water. Pour into mold. Allow to set for 12 hours.

Serve cold with Mayonnaise (see Index). Can be served with assorted hors d'oeuvres and sandwiches.

Leftover cooking liquid is an excellent base for pea or bean soup.

Wilted Dandelion Salad

- *Salade de Pissenlits*

    1 lb. dandelion greens
    6 slices bacon
    1 tbsp. bacon drippings
    ⅓ cup heavy cream
    2 eggs
    3 dashes black pepper
    3 dashes paprika
    1 tbsp. sugar
    4 tbsp. vinegar
      Salt to taste (careful: bacon may be salty)
    6 slices Canadian bacon, fried lightly
    6 boiled potatoes

Rub greens dry after washing. Arrange in salad bowl. Allow to crisp in refrigerator. Fry bacon until crisp. Take it out of the pan and place on absorbent paper. Break into little pieces.

Add bacon drippings to fat already in the pan. Pour in the cream over very low heat. Beat eggs, add seasonings, then sugar and vinegar. Pour into cream mixture, stirring constantly. Gradually increase heat and stir until dressing becomes thick like custard, taking good care not to let it curdle.

Sprinkle bacon over dandelion greens. Pour piping hot dressing over it. Serve at once with Canadian bacon and boiled potatoes. Serves 6.

WILTED LETTUCE: Substitute lettuce for dandelions in preceding recipe. Rub hard-cooked egg yolk through a sieve and sprinkle it over lettuce. Serves 6.

Apple Pockets

• *Rombosses*

> 1 recipe Pâte Brisée (see Index)
> 6 apples, peeled, cored and sliced thickly
> 1 egg, beaten
> ¼ cup rock candy sugar, pounded to pea-size pieces

Divide dough into six small loaves. Roll out each little loaf on well-floured pastry board to a square ¼-inch thick. Put slices from one apple in middle of each square. Fold over one corner; brush end with beaten egg. Stick second corner to it. Renew operation until four corners stick together on top.

Stud tops with rock candy sugar. Bake 30 minutes in moderate (350°) oven. Yield: 6 apple pockets.

Twelfth Day Cake

• *Bouname*

> 2 cups all-purpose flour
> 3 tsp. double-action baking powder
> ½ tsp. salt
> 3 tbsp. soft butter
> 1 egg, beaten
> ¼ cup honey
> ⅔ cup heavy cream
> ½ cup rock candy sugar pounded to pea-size pieces

NOTE: *Bouname* is the *patois* word for *bonhomme,* old man —i.e., one of the Three Kings.

Sift flour, baking powder and salt together in large mixing bowl. Add butter, egg, honey and heavy cream. Knead with the fingers until well mixed and smooth.

On a buttered baking sheet mold into the silhouette of a man with flowing robes, about 1 inch thick. Stud robe with rock candy sugar and reserve a piece for the eye.

Bake in quick moderate oven (375°) for 12 to 15 minutes. Serve cold on a board or wooden tray. Serves 6 to 8.

Rice Ring with Apples

- *Riz aux Pommes*

> 4 cups milk
> 3 tbsp. Vanilla Sugar (see Index)
> ¾ cup packaged precooked rice
> 4 egg yolks beaten with 2 tbsp. heavy cream
> 1 cup sugar
> Rind of ½ lemon, grated
> 2 tart apples
> 3 slices canned pineapple
> 6 glacé cherries
> 2 tbsp. light rum *or* kirsch
> 2 tbsp. apricot jam *or* marmalade

Bring milk to a boil, add Vanilla Sugar and rice. Transfer to double boiler. Cook ¾ hour stirring once in a while. When grains are completely soft remove from fire and blend in egg yolk mixture. Pour into ring mold. Allow to cool over some ice.

In saucepan make a syrup by combining and boiling together over high heat 1½ cups water, sugar and lemon rind. Peel, core and dice apples. Drop them into syrup and cook over moderate heat until glassy but still solid.

Meanwhile, unmold rice custard on a deep platter. Decorate with pineapples slices and cherries. When apples are done, remove from boiling syrup with a perforated spoon. Pile them in center of ring.

Add liqueur and jam to syrup and reduce quantity to ½ by boiling uncovered over high heat. Pour over rice ring and allow to get ice-cold before serving. Serves 4.

Rice Torte

- *Dorées de Mons*

> ⅓ recipe Pâte Brisée (see Index)
> 1 recipe Rice Custard (see Index)
> 2 egg yolks beaten with ½ cup cream

Place rolled-out Pâte Brisée in a 9-inch pie pan and prick bottom with a fork. Pour in Rice Custard and over it egg and cream mixture. Bake in quick moderate oven (375°) 40 minutes. Serves 6 to 8.

Macaroons from Beaumont

- *Macarons*

> ½ cup finely ground almonds
> 2⅔ cups sifted confectioners' sugar
> 1 tsp. vanilla extract
> 3 egg whites, unbeaten

Pound almonds and sugar together with a pestle until mixture forms a coarse paste and is well blended. Add vanilla extract and gradually work in the egg whites, adding only enough of the third white to make the paste soft. Heat the paste slightly in double boiler.

On a buttered cookie sheet lined with white paper drop the paste from the tip of a spoon. Allow to cool 1 hour, then bake in moderate (350°) oven 10 minutes.

Place paper on damp surface to remove macaroons easily. Stick them together two by two. When cold, place in airtight container. Yield: 2 dozen macaroons.

Liége, Dinant and the Ardennes

Liége, the earliest town of Continental Europe to be run along democratic principles, the scene of so many heroic fights to maintain civil liberty in the face of foreign domination, now spreads gracefully on both banks of the River Meuse, its suburbs reaching halfway up the surrounding hills. Until the 17th century, these hills were covered with vineyards yielding a gay little wine. Today, it is found in small quantities only, in private cellars around the town of Huy. The coal mines exploited in a limited way since 1400 A.D. have spread all over the countryside and have been drilled in depth. Aside from a few monuments left from the time Liége was the elegant capital of a flourishing principality, Liége has the appearance of an industrial city. It remains, however, the gateway to Belgium's vacationland, the lovely Ardennes, and a portal to good eating. The famed strawberries *du Thiers à Liége* grow at the foot of the slag heaps, the black earth giving them a deep red color and a special tartness. Between 7 and 9 o'clock in the morning *bottresses,* miners' wives sometimes dressed in picturesque costumes, chant their wares through the streets: *maquée,* a particularly fine-textured cottage cheese, and *cûtes peûres,* winter pears baked on great tin sheets after the bread has gone out of the bakers' ovens. When the glistening butter-rubbed skin of the pear is opened, the soft, pinkish meat and the special aroma reveal to the connoisseur that the pear was a true *Bergamotte.* Rice torten are to be found in all the bakers' windows. In the bourgeois houses, rich sauces cover delicate meats and fishes, and the finest wines imported from France are gathering dust in the cool brick cellars of the houses, for the Walloon is by nature a gourmet and spends much time in his selection of food and much of his money on vintage Burgundies.

By tradition, on New Year's day, children and beggars offer any passerby a thin, waferlike cake with a Roman name, *Nules.* The cake bears the imprint of a cross. Buying a *Nules* is a propitiatory gesture granting forgiveness for venial sins. At Christmastime, buckwheat pancakes and blood sausage are on every table. After supper on Christmas Eve, the good Liégeois visit with equal fervor the mangers in every church in town, the cafés where buxom torch singers emote to the tunes they sang thirty years ago, the theater of marionettes where Tchantches, a salty character out of Liége's fiery past, talks back unabashed to the great emperor, Charlemagne.

From Liége to the southernmost district of Belgium, the land rises and so does the tempo of speech, in the sing-song voice typical of the Walloon dialect. East of Liége are beautiful meadows, rich pastureland where the ancestor of American Limburger cheese, odoriferous *fromage de Herve,* can be enjoyed. The mountain streams are filled with trout and crawfish, which are featured on the menus of the excellent inns around Namur and Dinant. This last city has been famous since Medieval times for embossed copperwork called *dinanderies*. The quaint shops feature the pots, the molds, the pans, the great platters, the urns and the bellows which have become renowned all over the world. Collectors' items can still be found in antique shops together with prized glassware from Liége and Namur, where in Roman times master Venetian glass blowers once taught their trade to Belgian apprentices. Though different in shape from the Venetian, Walloon glassware, particularly that of the 17th and 18th centuries, has an airiness, a fragile beauty, which is greatly prized by connoisseurs.

Dinant, a sleepy little town today, was in the 15th century one of the largest market towns of the country. Heavily fortified with battlements and towers and protected by huge cliffs, it was a city which had endured and won 17 sieges and was considered impregnable. A rivalry with the copper workers from Bouvignes in the neighboring county was the pretext for its destruction. Charles the Bold, duke of Burgundy, burned the town. For seven long months one hundred workmen were employed, demolishing and leveling the rubble until no trace of the city was left. The animosity which the people of Dinant felt for those of Bouvignes is still perpetuated in *patois* songs:

> "Ki veigne, ki veigne
> S'il est d'Boveigne
> S'il est d'Dinant
> No l'ritchessrant . . ."

Past Dinant and on toward Bastogne lies the great forest, a paradise for hunters. In October, on the day of St. Hubert, the horses and hounds are blessed from the steps of the monastery of the patron saint of all hunters. This marks the official opening of the hunting season. Venison, game birds, wild boar abound. In many Ardennes farmyards, the young boar is still roasted on a spit, rubbed with mountain thyme, its flesh delicately tasting of the juniper berries and huckleberries boars are fond of eating.

Farther down, near Arlon, in the sandy soil of the Gaume, grow the lovely potatoes known as *corne di gatte,* goat's horns; reddish brown, ugly shaped, but marvelously light and floury when cooked. I once watched a farmer's wife fixing them in an earthen pot for her second breakfast. She fried a little bacon; as soon as it was crisp she crumbled it, while on an old plate she half mashed with her fork her snowy potatoes and then tossed them back into the pot. While the potatoes sizzled in the bacon fat, she began to talk to me about her cows until the smell of scorching fat brought her attention back to the pot. She made a great fuss about stirring the potatoes and then again let her thoughts wander to the stable while the potatoes got singed on the other side—but better potatoes I have never eaten.

Plum trees and hazelnut bushes thrive on the sandy soil of the Ardennes. Hazelnuts and potatoes are used in combination to make the most marvelous pancakes.

The Gaume is a scented country; in the shrub oak and hazelnut woods there hangs a smell of acid humus; the clearings are full of heather, the meadows fragrant with dwarf varieties of golden and white clover. Thyme creeps along the byways, while borage and chicory add a bright blue note. There are beehives in many backyards, the honey tasting of these plants and also of the buckwheat in the fields. But prevalent all year round, permeating the clothes of the people, is the scent of burning juniper wood. It comes from the smokehouses.

In almost every village there is a pigherder paid on a communal basis. A special breed of pigs is sent every morning to forage for acorns and mountain grass. At evening time, the hogs are brought back to the villages to the sound of a horn. Housewives open pigsty doors and call their hogs in individual shrill tones. The hogs come rolling down the hills on their short legs and fill the narrow streets with their grunting. It is quite a sight.

Jambon d'Ardennes, saucisson, smoked tenderloins and filets are justly famous. They are not cured with sugar, as in this country, but in brine and then smoked until quite dark and quite dry—drier than *prosciutto,* even darker than Westphalian ham, with a flavor at once pungent and mellow.

The peasant from Gaume is thrifty by necessity. With the exception of the peat bogs of the Fagnes, here is the poorest soil in Belgium. Yet in this corner, which rolls gently toward France, there is a *douceur de vivre.* People live slowly, comfortably. Snowbound much of the winter, they have time to enjoy great repasts, and although their land is poor they manage to achieve quiet prosperity. They still visit from one farmhouse to another on early winter eves and have bean or pea shelling parties, picking the vegetables from the dried, yellowed vines. Refreshments will be mulled wine or *pecquet,* a harsh gin made from potato and juniper berries, or the delicious *quetsch,* distilled from blue plums which grow abundantly in small orchards. This part of Belgium offers the most to the tourist. The scenery is lovely; the farmhouses of glistening granite or of pink adobe under pointed slate roofs designed to shed the heavy snows. The casinos of Spa and Namur are gay, the fine hotels and the inns offer good fishing, and in season big game hunting and wild boar hunting, a sport fast disappearing in Europe. The food is the best and the most varied in Belgium. The native wines, though smaller than Rhine wines, are pleasant and inexpensive.

Consommé St. Hubert

• *Consommé St. Hubert*

>   3 lbs. breast of venison
>   1 venison shank
>   1 marrow bone, cracked
>   2 onions
>   4 cloves
>   2 carrots
>   2 leeks
>   1 celery stalk
>   1 bay leaf
>   ⅛ tsp. powdered thyme
>   2 sprigs parsley
>   Pepper and salt to taste
>   3 tbsp. quick-cooking tapioca

GARNISH:

>   ½ cup claret
>   ½ cup precooked or canned lentils
>   ½ cup lean meat from breast, finely cut
>   1 cup mixed peas, carrots and celery

Cover meat with 4 quarts water. Add all ingredients except tapioca. Bring to a boil, simmer for 2 hours. Remove meats and vegetables. Line a colander with cheesecloth or toweling. Place a tray of ice cubes at bottom. Place colander over clean soup pot. Strain broth through it. Ice will remove all grease. Bring broth to a boil once more over high heat. Add tapioca and cook until liquid is reduced by half. Taste and correct seasoning.

10 minutes before serving add garnishes and cook until vegetables and meat are tender. Makes 8 cups.

Smoky Tomato Soup

- *Soupe aux Tomates*

  1 ham bone *or* smoked ham butt
  6 tomatoes
  2 yellow squash (large)
  5 sprigs parsley
  ½ bay leaf
  ⅛ tsp. powdered oregano
  ⅛ tsp. powdered thyme
  Pepper and salt to taste

Place ham bone or butt in a deep pot and cover with 3 quarts water. Bring to a boil, reduce heat and simmer 2 hours. Skim. Add remaining ingredients and simmer 1 hour.

Push through food mill. Taste and correct seasoning. Reheat and serve with croutons (see Index) or bite-size pieces of ham. Serves 4 to 6.

Cheese Appetizers

- *Fritots à la Liégeoise*

  ¼ cup soft bread crumbs
  1 cup grated parmesan cheese
  1 egg yolk
  ¼ tsp. prepared mustard
  Salt and cayenne pepper to taste
  1 egg white, stiffly beaten
  ½ cup dry bread crumbs (more or less)

Mix soft bread crumbs, cheese, egg yolk and seasonings. Fold in egg white. Shape into balls the size of a walnut. Roll in dry bread crumbs. Fry in deep fat (390°) until golden brown. Drain on absorbent paper. Serve hot. Yield: 10 to 12 balls.

Crawfish

• *Écrevisses à la nage*

    4 peppercorns, bruised
    Dusting cayenne pepper
    3 qts. Court-Bouillon (see Index)
  16 live crawfish

Add peppercorns and cayenne to Court-Bouillon and bring to a boil. Plunge crawfish into this boiling liquid and cook, uncovered, over high heat 10 minutes. Serve hot in liquid. Serves 4.

Galantine of Trout

• *Galantine de Truite*

    1 large lake trout (3 to 4 lbs.)
    1 slice of bread
  ½ lb. codfish, ground
    2 qts. milk
    4 truffles, chopped
    2 eggs, 1 raw, 1 hard-boiled
    Ground pepper, cayenne pepper and salt to taste
  ½ cup jellied chicken consommé, just beginning to set
    2 cups Mayonnaise (see Index)
    1 tsp. tomato purée
    1 small jar caviar for canapés

Split trout and remove backbone with sharp kitchen knife. Rub bread between palms of hands to get thick crumbs. Make a stuffing with ground codfish, bread crumbs, 1 tablespoon of the milk, chopped truffles and raw egg. Season with pepper, cayenne pepper and salt to taste.

Fill trout with stuffing. Roll in a cloth, tie the ends securely to keep in shape. Poach in salted milk for 20 minutes. Cool in poaching liquid.

Unpack trout. Arrange on bed of lettuce. Frost with consommé and garnish all around with small canapés of caviar, alternating with hard-cooked egg slices topped with Mayonnaise and a bit of truffle.

Serve with Mayonnaise mixed with tomato purée to make it pink. Serves 6.

Fisherman's Trout

- *La Truite du Pêcheur*

> 1 trout
> Pepper and salt to taste
> 1 tbsp. butter kneaded with 1 tsp. chopped fresh sorrel
> *or* ¼ tsp. dried sorrel

Slice trout down the middle and gut, leaving head and tail intact. Place on grill 6 inches from ash-covered coals of barbecue pit. When skin comes loose from grill turn trout and repeat procedure.

When done on both sides season with salt and pepper and add butter mixture on the inside.

Perfect accompaniments: thinly sliced cucumber with lemon juice and a new potato cooked in the skin. Serves 1.

I have often prepared this by the side of the stream on a fire built between three stones with a flat one white-hot on top on which to lay the trout, the potato boiled at the edge of the fire in a canteen.

With the frozen Danish trout available in most American cities at better fish markets, it makes an easy menu for an outdoor meal. Also, I have successfully replaced the trout with mackerel, using fennel tips or dill for flavoring.

Blue Trout with White Butter

- *Truite au Bleu, Beurre Blanc*

> 4 cups Court-Bouillon (see Index)
> 4 live trout

Have liquid boiling in a large, shallow pot. Place trout in it, reduce heat and poach until flesh of fish can be detached easily from bones at thickest point. The trout looks bright blue, and the tail is naturally curled toward the mouth.

SAUCE:

> 2 shallots *or* 1 small onion, bruised
> 3 sprigs parsley
> ½ cup tart white wine (we use Moselle)
> 1 tbsp. white vinegar
> ½ lb. butter
> Pepper and salt to taste
> Dusting of cayenne pepper

Place shallots, parsley, wine and vinegar in a saucepan. Boil over high heat, uncovered, until reduced in volume to ¼ cup. Remove from heat. Strain. Into clear liquid stir butter, 1 tablespoon at a time, creaming it until white. Place over very slow heat IF NECESSARY. This sauce should have the consistency of mayonnaise. Taste. Season with pepper and salt and dust with cayenne pepper.

Serve separately in a sauceboat. White butter is garnished with chopped truffle when available. Serves 4.

Casserole of Pike

- *Filets de Brochet Ménagère*

> 2 tbsp. butter
> 1 cup mushroom stems and pieces, chopped
> 1 tbsp. chopped parsley
> 4 pike (approximately 1 lb. each) cut in filets
> 1 cup dry white wine
>   Pepper and salt
> 1 tbsp. butter kneaded with 1 tbsp. flour
> 2 tbsp. butter

Butter generously the sides and bottom of a shallow casserole. In it place mushrooms, parsley and filets of pike. Cover with wine, season *lightly* with pepper and salt and bake covered in moderate (350°) oven 12 minutes, or until fish is tender.

Drain cooking liquid into a saucepan. Reduce liquid to half its volume by boiling uncovered over high heat. Add butter-flour mixture and allow to thicken by boiling 5 minutes, stirring constantly. Taste and correct seasoning. Melt remaining 2 tablespoons butter in sauce and pour over the filets. Serves 4 to 6.

Pike Dumplings with Bisque Sauce

• *Quenelles de Brochet la Gaichelle*

> 2 frozen African rock lobster tails
> 2 cups Court-Bouillon (see Index)
> 1½ cups Béchamel Sauce (see Index) made with liquid
>   in which lobster was poached
> 1 can crawfish bisque
> ½ cup heavy cream
> 1 jigger cognac
> 2 tbsp. sherry
> 1 cup sautéed mushrooms
>   Pepper and salt to taste
> 1 can pike dumplings *

Poach lobster tails for 17 minutes. Cut each tail down the back with a short, sharp knife, halving it lengthwise. Remove meat.

Make Béchamel Sauce and mix with bisque. Add cream, cognac, sherry and the mushrooms with pan juices to which 2 tablespoons water have been added. Add salt and pepper. Taste and correct seasoning.

Add lobster tails and dumplings. Heat thoroughly without boiling and serve with Steamed Rice (see Index) or toast points. May be prepared ahead of time and warmed in slow (300°) oven. Serves 4.

* Dumplings are imported from France and available at fancy food stores.

Spinach Noodles Arlonnaise

- *Nouilles Vertes à la Mode d'Arlon*

 ½ lb. spinach noodles
 2 slices white bread
 2 tbsp. butter
   Pepper and salt to taste
 4 poached eggs
 8 slices smoked ham *or* prosciutto

Place noodles in boiling water. Add salt and cook for 15 minutes without a cover. Drain in strainer and rinse quickly under a stream of cold water.

Crumble bread by rubbing it between the palms of your hands, so as to make thick crumbs. Fry crumbs in butter until golden brown. Meanwhile replace noodles in pot over low flame with a teaspoonful of butter. Use pepper mill over noodles. Add bread crumbs. Mix together. Place in center of dish and surround with poached eggs alternating with thin slices of smoked ham. Serves 4.

Noodles with Sauerkraut

• *Nouilles à la Choucroute*

> 1 lb. fresh sauerkraut
> ½ cup dry white wine (we use Moselle)
> 6 juniper berries
> ⅛ tsp. nutmeg
> ½ bay leaf
> 2 cloves
> Dusting of cayenne pepper
> Pepper and salt to taste
> 1 lb. wide noodles
> 1 tbsp. butter
> 2 tbsp. bread crumbs, toasted
> 1½ cup chopped smoked ham *or* prosciutto
> 3 eggs
> 1 cup milk
> Pepper and salt to taste

Bring sauerkraut and seasonings to a boil in wine. Simmer over low heat for 20 minutes. Meanwhile, boil noodles rapidly in open pot for 18 minutes. Drain in colander, wash with cold water and drain again. Thickly butter a 1-quart mold and sprinkle with bread crumbs. In the mold alternate layer of noodles and layer of ham until mold is ¾ full. Beat eggs until well mixed, add milk and pour into mold. Cover with aluminum foil and bake in slow oven (300°) 1 hour. Unmold. Drain sauerkraut; make a ring of it around the noodles. Serves 4.

Carrot Mold

- *Pottée aux Carottes*

    6 large carrots, thinly sliced
    6 large potatoes, cubed
    ¼ cup heavy cream
    1 egg yolk
    3 tbsp. butter
      Pepper and salt to taste

Boil carrots and potatoes together in salted water until soft. Drain carefully, then put through food mill. Add other ingredients. Beat well with wire whisk or electric blender. Press purée into buttered 1-quart pudding mold. Bake in hot oven (450°) for 15 minutes. To serve, invert on a platter. Serves 4 to 6.

Potato and Celery Mold

- *Pottée Gaumaise*

    12 stalks celery
     1 leek
     6 large potatoes, cubed
     4 tbsp. butter
     2 egg yolks
     ½ cup grated Switzerland Swiss cheese

Carefully remove threads from celery stalks. Boil celery. leek and potatoes together in salted water until soft. Drain carefully, then put through food mill. Add 2 tablespoons of the butter, egg yolks and 4 tablespoons of the cheese. Beat well with wire whisk or electric blender.

Butter 1-quart pudding mold with remaining butter. Pour

mixture into mold and bake in moderate oven (350°) 15 minutes. Unmold on ovenproof platter. Sprinkle with remaining cheese and brown lightly under the broiler. Serves 4 to 6.

Smothered Potatoes

- *Pommes de Terre à l'Etouffée*

    6 medium-sized potatoes
  ½ cup butter
  2 tbsp. dry white wine (we use Moselle)
    Salt and pepper to taste
  ¼ onion, diced (optional)
    Chopped parsley

Peel and wash the potatoes. Do not dry them. Cut in four pieces. Melt butter in a flameproof casserole; add potatoes, wine, pepper, salt and onion. Cover tightly. Cook on slow heat for ¾ hour. Remove cover. Turn up the heat to high. Shake pot gently while liquid evaporates and potatoes get golden. Serve in the casserole. Sprinkle with chopped parsley. Serves 4.

Hot String Bean Salad

- *Salade Liégeoise*

  4 large potatoes
  1 lb. string beans
  1 heaping tbsp. butter
  1 cup beef broth
  ¼ lb. sliced bacon
  1 scallion, finely minced
  ⅛ tsp. dried savory
  Pepper to taste
  2 tbsp. vinegar
  ½ lb. Canadian bacon

Peel and wash potatoes; slice thickly. Break string beans in pieces two inches long.

In an earthenware flameproof casserole melt butter and add potatoes and string beans together. Moisten with beef broth. Season to taste and cover. Simmer over slow heat for 1¼ hours, approximately. Make sure potatoes and string beans are well done.

Broil sliced bacon. Drain on absorbent paper and break into small pieces. Reserve ½ cup bacon fat. Heat it thoroughly and add minced scallion, savory, pepper and vinegar. Mix well with a wooden spoon. Pour over string beans and potatoes in casserole and as a last touch, add bacon.

Toss like a salad and serve surrounded by fried Canadian bacon. Serves 4.

Brussels Sprouts with Green Grapes

- *Choux de Bruxelles Véronique*

    1½ cups chicken broth *or* stock
    4 packages frozen Brussels sprouts
    1 cup green Malaga grapes, cut in two & seeded *
    1 tbsp. butter
    Dusting of white pepper

Bring broth to a boil in flameproof casserole. Place frozen sprouts in it and bring again to a boil. Reduce the heat. Simmer sprouts for 15 minutes. Add grapes and simmer 7 to 10 minutes more. Add butter. Dust with pepper. Taste and correct seasoning. Serve in casserole. Serves 6.

String Beans Ardennaise

- *Haricots Verts*

    3 slices Canadian bacon, minced
    1 onion, minced
    2 tbsp. butter
    2 boxes frozen string beans, French style
    Pepper and salt
    ⅛ tsp. summer savory
    ¼ cup consommé
    1 egg yolk, beaten
    ½ tsp. cornstarch
    2 tbsp. heavy cream
    1 tbsp. chopped parsley
    8 slices smoked ham *or* prosciutto, warmed and slightly fried in 1 tsp. butter

* Along the River Moselle, where the Belgian vineyards are, the casserole is lined with grape leaves before cooking process. I recommend this procedure. Sprayed leaves must be soaked overnight before use.

Sauté bacon and onion in butter until very lightly browned. Add frozen beans and seasonings. Moisten with consommé Cook over low heat for half an hour. Combine egg yolk, cornstarch and cream and add to beans. Allow to thicken slightly.

Sprinkle with parsley and serve surrounded with rolled up ham. Serves 4.

Smoked Loin of Pork with Sauerkraut

- *Kastlerribchen*

    1 lb. fresh sauerkraut
    8 juniper berries, crushed
    ½ cup tart white wine (we use Moselle)
    ½ bay leaf
    4 peppercorns, bruised
    4 chops from a smoked loin of pork

Place all ingredients in a flameproof casserole. Bring to a boil. Reduce heat and simmer, covered, 45 minutes, or until chops are tender.

Drain. Serve with mashed potatoes. Serves 4.

Smoked Ham in a Blanket

- *Jambon d'Ardennes en Croûte*

    1 small, precooked smoked ham *
    2 2-crust size recipes pie crust
    ½ cup fine Madeira wine

* Smithfield country ham may be used, but Westphalian or Ardennes hams are more appropriate, if available.

Remove skin and most of the fat from ham. Roll out pie crust in one large square and wrap the ham in it so that seams are under the ham. On the top part of the crust cut an opening in a flower design for the steam to escape, and also perforate the dough lengthwise. Place on a cookie sheet and bake in slow oven (300°) 1 hour and 20 minutes.

When done pour wine under the crust with a funnel. To cut ham, break the crust at center line and remove from sides of ham like a shell. Divide crust into pieces and serve with the meat. Serve this with prepared baby food purée of peas, seasoned to taste, and a Madeira Sauce (see below). This makes a spectacular buffet dish. Serves 10 to 12.

MADEIRA SAUCE:

> 3 cups light Béchamel Sauce (see Index) made with beef consommé
> 1 cup Madeira wine
> ¾ cup tomato purée

Combine all ingredients and serve hot. Makes 4 cups.

Veal Kidneys Liége Style

- *Rognons de Veau Liégeoise*

> 4 veal kidneys
> 2 tbsp. butter
> 4 chopped juniper berries
> Salt and pepper to taste
> 1 tbsp. Burgundy wine

Cut off most of the fat around the kidneys, leaving only a thin layer. Cut kidneys in thick slices. Heat butter to sizzling point in a flameproof casserole. Add kidneys and berries. Brown over medium heat, covered, turning meat several times.

When done (about 15 minutes) add salt and pepper to taste and wine. Serves 2.

Black Sausage

* *Boudin de Noël*

> 1 lb. ground pork
> ¾ pt. pig's blood
> 2 lbs. white cabbage, boiled in a great deal of water then drained and put through a sieve
> ½ cup onions, chopped fine
> 1 tbsp. salt
> ⅛ tsp. pepper

Proceed as for White Sausage (see Index).

This is delicious sautéed, with apple rings powdered with brown sugar.

The Belgian peasants eat it cold, sliced, with well-buttered black bread.

Calves' Brains and Potato Salad

• *Cervelles de Veau Arlonnaise*

> 2 calves' brains
> 1 recipe Court-Bouillon (see Index)
> 1 cup Mayonnaise (see Index)
> ½ tsp. prepared mustard
> 1 dusting cayenne pepper
> ⅛ tsp. cumin powder *or* ¼ tsp. celery seed
> ⅛ tsp. ground pepper
> 2 tsp. lemon juice
> 1 hard-cooked egg, sliced
> 4 gherkins, sliced
> 1 recipe Potato Salad Ardennaise (see following recipe)

Remove skin covering brains. Soak brains for 15 minutes in cold water. Poach ½ hour in Court-Bouillon. Drain and allow to cool. Place in refrigerator until very cold. Slice into pieces ½-inch thick. To Mayonnaise, add mustard, cayenne, cumin powder or celery seed, ground pepper and lemon juice. Blend.

Spread sliced brains lightly with Mayonnaise on both sides. Arrange in a ring on a platter. Cover with rest of Mayonnaise. Decorate with sliced egg and gherkins. Fill center of ring with Potato Salad Ardennaise. Serves 4.

Potato Salad Ardennaise

- *Salade de Pommes de Terre*

> 4 cups potatoes, boiled, peeled and sliced thinly
> Juice of 1 lemon
> 1 cup French Dressing (more or less) (see Index)
> ½ cup diced smoked ham *or* prosciutto
> 1 tsp. chervil, powdered or freshly chopped
> 1 tsp. chives, powdered or freshly chopped
> 1 tsp. parsley, powdered or freshly chopped

Sprinkle potatoes with lemon juice. Mix potatoes, dressing and ham thoroughly. Place in refrigerator and allow dressing to soak into potatoes for 1 hour. Add more dressing if necessary and correct seasoning to taste. Before serving sprinkle top of salad with herbs. Serves 4.

Partridge and Cabbage

- *Perdrix aux Choux*

> 2 partridges
> Pepper and salt, light-handedly
> ½ lb. bacon, cut and diced
> 1 Savoy cabbage
> ½ lb. carrots, sliced thickly
> 1 turnip, diced
> ⅛ tsp. thyme
> ⅛ tsp. mace
> 2 cups consommé *or* stock
> ½ cup flour

Wash and dry partridges inside and out. Season. Fry bacon in a pan. Drain on absorbent paper and reserve. In drippings, brown birds on all sides. Line a large casserole with some cabbage leaves. Add carrots and turnip. Place partridges in center. Cover with bacon and more cabbage leaves. Season with thyme and mace. Add consommé. Cover casserole. Make a paste with flour and a little water. Seal pot with a strip of this dough over opening between pot and cover. Bake in hot oven (425°) for 1 to 2 hours, depending upon age of birds. Serves 4.

Partridge with Beans

- *Perdrix Braisée aux Haricots*

        ½ lb. dried navy beans
        2 cups chicken broth
        2 partridges
        ½ stick butter
        ½ cup Canadian bacon, diced
        1 medium onion, sliced
        ½ clove garlic, crushed
        ½ cup dry white wine
        ¼ lb. salami, diced
          Salt and pepper to taste
        1 tbsp. chopped parsley

Take a large casserole. In it simmer dried navy beans for 1½ hours in 2 cups chicken broth, adding enough water to cover. Check the amount of liquid during cooking time. If necessary add more *boiling* water.

Meanwhile, cut partridges in 4 pieces. In a large skillet brown them rapidly in butter. Add Canadian bacon, onion, garlic, white wine, salami. Season to taste. Transfer foods from skillet into casserole. Allow to simmer for ½ hour or until partridges are tender, depending on birds' age.

Taste and correct seasoning. Sprinkle parsley over the top and serve right from casserole. Makes 4 generous portions.

Goose or Duck Visé Style

· *Canard à l'Instar de Visé*

> A goose or duck
> ½ lb. butter
> 3 tbsp. flour, sifted
> ½ cup cold water
> 1 cup milk
> Pepper, salt, nutmeg to taste
> 2 egg yolks
> ½ tsp. garlic powder

Roast bird in covered pan in hot oven (475°) with giblets. Roasting time: about 15 minutes to the pound. Melt butter in a medium-sized double boiler. Stir in flour, then cold water, then milk, stirring rapidly with a wooden spoon while mixture thickens over slow heat. Simmer 15 minutes. Sauce should be smooth and have the consistency of a cream sauce. Season rather highly. Remove from fire. Add egg yolks. Keep hot in double boiler away from heat.

Just before serving, carve bird and arrange it on a heated platter. Remove grease from pan. Add ¼ cup cold water to glaze in bottom of roasting pan and bring to a boil. Mix this juice with white sauce and add garlic powder. Pour over duck or goose and serve very hot with braised celery, broiled tomatoes and fried potatoes. Serves 6.

Pheasant or Guinea Hen Ardennaise

- *Faisan ou Pintade*

> 1 pheasant hen 2½ to 3 lbs.
> Pepper and salt to taste
> 3 tbsp. butter
> 1 3-oz. package cream cheese
> 8 juniper berries
> ½ cup diced bacon, raw
> ¼ cup cognac *or* Quetsch if available
> 1 cup heavy cream

Wash and dry pheasant. Reserve liver. Simmer giblets in ½ cup boiling water. Sprinkle pheasant with pepper and salt, inside and out. Rub butter on skin of bird. Place cream cheese in cavity. Roast in hot oven (400°) with berries for about 1½ hours. Add liver and bacon in the last 20 minutes. Cut bird into four portions, giving a little of the breast to each guest. Arrange on a platter. Keep hot.

Pour giblet broth into pan drippings and with liver put in electric blender or through a fine sieve. Bring to a boil. Add cognac, remove from heat and thicken with heavy cream. Correct seasoning and pour over four portions of pheasant. Serves 4.

Roast Pheasant with Sauerkraut

- *Faisan à la Choucroute*

```
    1 lb. fresh sauerkraut
    ½ cup tart white wine (we use Moselle)
    6 juniper berries, bruised
    ½ bay leaf
    4 peppercorns, bruised
    1 hen pheasant (2½ to 3 lbs.)
    1 3-oz. package cream cheese
      Pepper and salt to taste
    3 tbsp. butter
      Cheesecloth square
```

In a flameproof casserole, bring sauerkraut to a boil with wine and seasonings. Reduce heat and simmer 45 minutes.

Wash and dry pheasant inside and out. Place cream cheese inside cavity. Season with pepper and salt. Rub butter into cheesecloth and cover pheasant with it. Place in roasting pan and roast undisturbed in hot (450°) oven 1 hour, or until done.

Discard cheese. Drain sauerkraut. Carve the pheasant and place the pieces on a bed of sauerkraut. Garnish with watercress. Serve pan juices in sauceboat. Serves 4.

Deer Chops with Gin

- *Côtes de Chevreuil au Genièvre*

      2 tbsp. butter
      8 deer chops
      7 heart-shaped croutons (see Index)
    ¼ cup Dutch gin
      2 juniper berries, crushed
      1 tsp. lemon juice
      3 tbsp. bottled Escoffier Sauce Diable
    ½ cup heavy cream

Melt butter in heavy skillet and bring to bubbling point. Add chops and sauté till golden brown. Remove chops to a heated platter and arrange them in a ring, slipping a crouton between each chop.

Pour gin in skillet. Set it aflame and stir to deglaze the skillet. Add the crushed juniper berries, lemon juice and Sauce Diable. Reduce heat and stir in the heavy cream. Pour over chops. Serve with a tart applesauce and puréed chestnuts. Makes 4 generous portions.

Deer Steaks Piquante

- *Biftecks de Chevreuil, Sauce Piquante*

    1½ cups Sauce Piquante (see following recipe)
      2 tbsp. butter
      4 individual deer steaks, cut ½ inch thick

Prepare sauce and keep hot over low heat.

Place butter in frying pan over high heat until it sizzles. Brown steaks in butter on both sides until rare, medium or well done, according to taste. Rare—3 to 4 minutes each side; medium—5 minutes each side; well done—6 minutes each side.

Place steaks on heated platter. Pour sauce over them. Serve with Brussels Sprouts and Chestnuts (see Index) or mashed potatoes. Serves 4.

Sauce Piquante

- *Sauce Piquante*

  ¼ cup white wine
  ¼ cup cider vinegar
  1 tbsp. chopped shallots *or* onion
  1½ cups Sauce Espagnole (see Index)
  2 tsp. chopped gherkins
  1 tsp. chopped parsley
  ⅛ tsp. dried tarragon
  (1 short sprig of tarragon, chopped, is better)

Boil together over high heat white wine, vinegar and shallots until reduced to ½ the volume. Mix with Sauce Espagnole. Simmer over medium heat for 10 minutes, stirring once in a while. Remove from heat, add gherkins and herbs.

Makes approximately 1½ cups. May also be served with ham or pork chops.

Boar's Ham, Sweet-Sour

- *Jambon de Marcassin à l'Aigre-Doux*

> 1 fresh ham from *young* wild boar
> Pepper and salt to taste
> Liquid from a can of sour cherries
> 2 cups Sauce Espagnole (see following recipe)
> Sour cherries, drained
> 1 tbsp. grated orange rind
> 2 tbsp. wine vinegar
> 2 tbsp. butter

Remove all but a thin layer of fat from the ham. Season with pepper and salt. Bake 3 hours in quick moderate oven (375°). Remove ham from pan and keep hot in the oven.

Pour off all fat from roasting pan. Place pan over high heat. Deglaze sides and bottom by stirring cherry liquid into it. Add Sauce Espagnole, cherries, orange rind and vinegar. Boil over high heat until sauce is reduced to ⅔ original volume. Taste and correct seasoning. Finish with butter.

Slice ham and place on serving platter. Pour half of sauce over it and surround with unsweetened applesauce. Serve remaining sauce from a sauceboat. Serves 4 to 6, generously.

Sauce Espagnole

> 2 tbsp. canned tomato purée
> 3 tbsp. flour
> 3 tbsp. butter
> 2½ cups beef consommé
> ½ bay leaf
> ⅛ tsp. powdered thyme
> ½ tsp. onion salt
> Pepper to taste
> 2 tbsp. white wine

Prepare tomato purée by drying it out in slow to medium oven (325°) on a piece of foil until it takes on a brownish color (about 15 minutes). In a small frying pan place flour, dry, over high heat. Stir with a fork. Allow to burn evenly to a peanut color. Remove from heat and continue stirring until pan has cooled slightly.

In saucepan melt butter and add browned flour, stirring rapidly with a whisk. Moisten with a few drops of consommé. While stirring, gradually add all consommé. Add herbs and season to taste. Mix in dried tomato purée. Allow to boil over high heat, stirring occasionally, until sauce is reduced to 2 cups in volume. As the sauce thickens, stir more frequently. Add wine. Makes 2 cups.

This sauce, to be used as a base for all brown gravies, keeps 2 weeks in a covered jar in the refrigerator. Recipe may be doubled. Freezes very well.

Roast Hare Back or Filet of Venison

• *Râble de Lièvre– Filet de Chevreuil*

> 1 hare back *or* filet of venison, marinated 12 hours
> 12 slices bacon
> ½ cup marinating liquid, strained
> ½ cup Sauce Espagnole (see preceding recipe)
> 4 tbsp. Escoffier Sauce Diable
> 4 tbsp. currant jelly
> 1 cup heavy cream

MARINATING LIQUID: Blend together and pour over meat

> 2 cups red wine
> ¼ cup cooking oil
> 3 onions, sliced
> 8 peppercorns, bruised
> 1 bay leaf
> ⅛ tsp. thyme

Dry meat thoroughly. Place in roasting pan and cover with bacon. Roast hare back in open pan for 1½ hours in a preheated hot oven (400°). Filet must be roasted 40 minutes in a very hot oven (475°).

Remove meat from pan. Keep hot in open oven. Pour off all the fat from the roasting pan. Place the pan over high heat and deglaze sides and bottom by stirring marinating liquid into it. Add Sauce Espagnole, Sauce Diable and jelly. Taste and correct seasoning, which should be sharp. Boil for 3 minutes. Remove from fire. Stir in cream.

Slice meat. Place on serving platter. Pour half of sauce over meat. Serve remaining sauce in sauceboat. Serve with Glazed Apples (see following recipe). Serves 4 to 6.

Glazed Apples

- *Pommes en Belle-vue*

> 6 medium-sized apples, peeled and cored
> 1 tbsp. Vanilla Sugar (see Index)
> ⅔ cup apple cider
> 1 cup Currant Jelly, melted (see Index)

Dust apples with sugar. Add cider. Bake in slow oven (300°) 35 minutes, basting several times with juice. Test apples with a fork; they are done when they are soft inside but still hold their shape.

Mix remaining juice in bottom of baking dish with jelly and glaze apples with this mixture.

Serve cold with game, or as a dessert with whipped cream. Serves 6.

Belgian Cottage Cheese

- *Mâquée*

> 2 qts. milk (unpasteurized is best)

Pour milk in earthen casserole. Cover with a folded towel. Leave it on side of the stove or in any warm place for 12 hours. By that time curds will have dropped to the bottom of the casserole.

Pour off all the water. Place a cheesecloth inside a bread basket and pour the curds into it. Place basket on a bowl to drip conveniently and store in refrigerator until well drained.

Belgian cottage cheese is turned out in the shape of the basket and cheesecloth removed very gently. Makes 2 cups. Eat with buttered Buckwheat Bread (see Index).

Fontainebleau Dessert

- *Coeur à la Crème*

Start 1 day ahead.

>2 cups Mâquée (see preceding recipe) *or* cottage cheese
>2 cups sour cream
>1 tbsp. Vanilla Sugar (see Index)
>1 pt. fresh strawberries *or* 1 jar Currant Jelly (see Index)
>Bread basket
>Cheesecloth

Place cheese, sour cream and sugar in a bowl. Blend, then beat until smooth.

Line bread basket or, if you have one, special heart-shaped basket, with cheesecloth. Pour mixture into it. Place in refrigerator over dish and allow to drip 24 hours.

Turn out on a platter and garnish with berries or jelly. Serve with Buckwheat Bread (see following recipe) or French bread. Serves 4 to 6.

Buckwheat Bread from the Ardennes

- *Pain de Sarrasin*

Starter:

>½ envelope dry yeast softened in ¼ cup lukewarm water
>1½ tbsp. sugar
>½ tsp. salt
>¼ cup rye flour
>¼ cup buckwheat flour
>¼ cup all-purpose flour

Dissolve softened yeast in 2 cups lukewarm water. Add all ingredients and blend well together. Cover and allow to stand ½ day at room temperature, stirring mixture down 3 times.

To make dough:

> ½ cup lukewarm water
> 1 cup starter
> 2 tbsp. honey
> 1 cup rye flour *
> 1 cup buckwheat flour *
> 1 cup all-purpose flour
> 2 tbsp. butter, melted

Add water to starter, then add all ingredients except butter. Knead well until dough is smooth. Grease bowl with half of butter, put dough in bowl and grease top of dough with remaining butter. Cover bowl with towel and set in warm place to rise until almost double in bulk—1 to 1½ hours. Punch dough down. Let rise, covered, again until double—about ½ hour. Let dough rest 10 minutes.

Shape into 2 oval loaves about 2½ inches high. Place on greased cookie sheet. Cover and let rise until doubled, about ¾ to 1 hour. Cut a lengthwise slit about ½ inch deep in top of each loaf. Brush with milk. Bake in preheated (400°) oven for 35 to 45 minutes, until loaf has a hollow sound when tapped. Makes 2 loaves.

* Rye and buckwheat flours may be purchased from specialty food shops and health food shops.

Buckwheat Pancakes

- *Bouquettes*

> ½ cup raisins
> ⅔ cup buckwheat flour
> ⅓ cup all-purpose flour
> 1 tsp. baking powder
> ½ tsp. salt
> 3 tbsp. sugar
> 3 eggs, well beaten
> 1¾ cups milk
> 2 tbsp. melted butter
> Butter for frying pancakes

Soak raisins in boiling water until plump. Drain on absorbent paper; reserve. Blend together all other ingredients and stir vigorously until batter is smooth; add raisins.

Heat a 9-inch frying pan (cast aluminum always rubbed with oil and never washed, and kept exclusively for pancakes is best) over high heat until butter sizzles at the touch. Drop into it ½ tablespoon butter. Shake pan to spread it, then ladle in about 2 tablespoons of batter. Grasp pan while doing this. and rotate, to spread batter. Fry until dry on top. Turn quickly with a spatula. To get an even golden color on reverse side, hold pan about an inch above heat and shake pan so that pancake slides a little back and forth and does not stick. Lift one edge gently with spatula, and when golden slide onto hot platter. Use ½ tablespoon butter per pancake. Pile cakes on top of each other, keeping them in warm (225°) open oven. Serve hot. Makes about 16 pancakes.*

* Pancakes freeze well when tightly wrapped in paper, foil or plastic pie containers. Or they may be made a day ahead, at leisure. To use, lightly butter pancake pan, place pancakes in it, cover with foil and heat through in warm (250°) oven.

Pancakes Gaumaise

- *Crèpes aux Avelines*

        3 medium potatoes
        ½ cup milk
        6 eggs
        ½ cup flour (scant)
        2 tbsp. Vanilla Sugar (see Index)
        ¼ cup heavy cream (generous)
        2 tbsp. butter, melted
        ½ cup chopped, blanched hazelnuts
        ¼ lb. butter for frying pancakes (more or less)

Boil the potatoes in skins in unsalted water. Peel and mash them with milk. Beat until smooth, adding eggs one at a time. Blend in flour, Vanilla Sugar, cream, 2 tablespoons melted butter and hazelnuts. Beat well.

Fry pancakes in butter according to preceding recipe (Buckwheat Pancakes).

Serve with Vanilla Sugar. Makes 16 pancakes.

Applesauce Soufflé

- *Soufflé aux Pommes*

        1 cup unsalted Béchamel Sauce (see Index)
        4 egg yolks
        1 tbsp. cream
        2 cups applesauce previously drained of juice in colander
        2 tbsp. rum *or* apple brandy
        5 egg whites, beaten stiff but not dry

Preheat oven to 375°. Remove Béchamel from heat. Add egg yolks and cream. Stir in applesauce and liqueur. Fold in egg whites. Pour into buttered 2-quart soufflé dish.

Place dish in pan of hot water and bake in quick moderate oven (375°) for 35 minutes or until well browned and puffed. Serve at once. Serves 6.

Baked Pears

- *Cûtes Peures*

> 8 large Seckel pears *or* 4 winter pears
> 4 tbsp. butter
> Vanilla Sugar (see Index)

Rub skin of pears with butter. Place on a cookie sheet and bake in slow oven (300°) for 45 minutes or until soft. Sprinkle heavily with Vanilla Sugar. Eat hot or cold. Serves 4.

Nun's Fritters

- *Pets de Nonne*

> ½ cup milk
> ⅛ tsp. salt
> ¼ lb. butter
> 1 cup sifted flour, diluted with ¾ cup water
> 3 eggs, well beaten
> 1 tsp. vanilla extract

Heat milk with salt and butter. At boiling point add flour-water mixture. Beat in eggs and vanilla.

Drop spoonfuls of the paste into deep fat (390°) and cook until golden brown. Drain on absorbent paper. Serve hot, sprinkled with Vanilla Sugar (see Index). Serves 4.

Coûques de Dinant

Start 2 days ahead *
>   2 cups buckwheat honey, warm
>   4 cups flour (more or less)

(Absorbency of honey varies with quality and weather conditions. It is therefore impossible to give exact measurements of flour.)

Put honey in mixing bowl. Gradually work in as much flour as honey will hold to make a stiff paste. Roll out between 2 sheets of waxed paper to ½-inch thickness. Cover. Allow to stand 2 days at room temperature; it will rise slightly; then cut out with the edge of a 6-inch bowl. If you wish, use floured embossed rolling pin to press in designs, or old wooden gingerbread molds. Bake in slow oven (300°) for 25 minutes or until light brown, almost yellow.

Will keep indefinitely in airtight container.

Makes 8 to 10 6-inch cakes.

* These cakes are hard and should be dunked when eaten. They have been a specialty of the city of Dinant since the Middle Ages. They are, upon analysis, the closest thing to the Biblical cake of flour and honey. Yemenites and Samaritans of Israel still make similar ones today, as do North African tribesmen. The cereal from which the flour is ground may vary from country to country, but this cake is universal wherever honey and cereals are to be found.

Rice Torte

- *Tarte Liégeoise*

> 1 recipe Sand Torte Pastry (see Index)
> 1 cup crushed macaroons
> 2 tbsp. rum diluted with 2 tbsp. water
> 2 cups Rice Custard (see Index)
> 2 egg yolks
> 1 whole egg beaten with ¼ cup heavy cream

Preheat oven to 375°. Line 10-inch spring form pan with pastry according to recipe. Sprinkle macaroons with rum-water mixture and distribute over pastry.

When basic Rice Custard is ready, add egg yolks and allow to thicken for 2 minutes. Do not boil. Pour over macaroons in unbaked torte. Cover with egg-cream mixture. Bake at 375° 45 minutes. Yield: 8 portions.

Strawberry Torte Chantilly

- *Tarte aux Fraises Chantilly*

> 1 recipe Sand Torte Pastry (see Index)
> 1 qt. fresh strawberries
> ½ cup strained strawberry jam diluted with 2 tbsp. boiling water
> ½ pt. heavy cream, whipped with 2 tbsp. Vanilla Sugar (see Index)

Preheat oven to 375°. Pat pastry on bottom of 10-inch spring form pan and 1 inch up sides. Place a layer of dried peas or beans in shell to keep bottom level. Bake 12 to 15 minutes.

Place hulled berries, bottoms down, in shell. Glaze with diluted jam and place 3 minutes in oven.

When ready to serve, decorate with whipped cream around edges and in center. Serves 6.

Belgian Brioche

- *Coûque de Visé*

  1 package dry yeast
  ¼ cup lukewarm water
  1 tsp. granulated sugar
  1 cup flour (more or less)
  4 cups sifted all-purpose flour
  ½ lb. butter, softened
  2 tbsp. granulated sugar
  ½ tsp. salt
  4 eggs
  ¾ cup milk
  ½ cup rock candy sugar, pounded to approximately pea
      size
  1 egg yolk, beaten

Soften yeast in water. Add sugar. To this mixture add 1 cup flour or enough to make a soft dough that can be worked into a ball. Put the ball into a buttered bowl, cover and allow to rise in a warm place until double in bulk.

Measure 2 cups of the sifted, all-purpose flour. Place in a large mixing bowl. Add ¼ pound of the butter, granulated sugar, salt, 2 eggs and ½ cup of the milk. Make a smooth paste. Add remaining flour, butter, 2 eggs, milk and ¼ cup of the rock candy sugar. Mix and knead until the paste is smooth and no longer sticky—adding flour if necessary. Beat the paste vigorously. Incorporate the paste with the ball of dough that has risen. Knead the mass long and well, but not so vigorously as before. Place dough in buttered bowl. Cover with a towel and allow to rise 2 to 2½ hours or until double in bulk. Punch it down and allow to stand overnight in refrigerator.

Use two 4 x 4 Pyrex bowls for the mold. Shape the dough into 2 balls, each large enough to half-fill a bowl; reserve enough to make 2 small, nut-sized balls. Make a crossways incision in the tops of the larger balls, then insert a smaller ball in each to make the heads of the brioches. Stud with remaining rock candy sugar. Cover the molds and allow to rise until double their bulk in a warm place. Brush with egg yolk. Bake in a hot oven (450°) until brown and shiny, 50 to 60 minutes. Makes 2 brioches.

Cool Currant Jelly

• *Gelée de Groseilles à Froid*

1½ lbs. sugar per lb. of currants
To every 5 lbs. currants, add ½ lb. raspberries

Wash fruit. Place it, stems and all, in jelly bag or cotton kitchen towel. Squeeze fruit over copper or stainless steel pot; for a clear jelly do not squeeze too hard. Repeat until all fruit is used.

Add sugar; stir. Cover with piece of glass and expose to sunshine for 6 hours, stirring every hour. Skim if necessary before placing in sterile glasses. Cover.

This jelly is more perishable than regular currant jelly; a

little less solid, too; but infinitely more delicate and fresh tasting.

Huckleberry Jam

- *Confiture de Myrtilles*

  4 cups huckleberries
  4 cups sugar
  Juice of 2 lemons
  1 tsp. grated lemon rind
  Cheesecloth bag with lemon seeds

Place berries in large stainless steel pot. Bruise them lightly with potato masher. Add sugar, lemon juice, rind and bag of seeds. Place over medium heat and allow most of the sugar to melt. Increase heat and bring to a rolling boil; cook for 15 to 20 minutes.

To judge if jam is jelling, place skimmer in the pot. Lift high. Last drops of jam should flake s owly from skimmer. Skim thoroughly. Pour into sterile jars, stirring each jar with a spoon to make sure fruit is evenly distributed. Seal with paraffin. Makes 8 6-ounce glasses.

Blackberry Jam

- *Confiture de Mûres*

Proceed as in Huckleberry Jam (see preceding recipe), substituting orange juice and grated orange rind for the lemon rind and juice.

Strawberry or Wild Strawberry Jam

• *Confiture de Fraises*

Proceed as for Huckleberry Jam (see Index), omitting grated rind. Use juice of 2 lemons for an unusual, bright color.

$\mathcal{B}$russels

FROM THE FARTHEST POINTS of Belgium, fresh vegetables, cheeses, fish and game reach the capitol by rail or road in less than four hours. The central open air market, which is held from dawn until 8:00 A.M. behind the main post office, is a sight for hungry people. The tenderest veal from Flanders, the freshest fish from Ostend, the venison and smoked hams from the Ardennes, the fine fruit from Tongeren, the spices and exotic Congolese produce just off the ships at Antwerp, find their way to wonderful restaurants.

The old streets in the heart of town have names redolent of good food: rue Montagne aux Herbes Potagères, rue aux Choux, rue des Navets, rue Marché aux Poulets. . . .

All over town there are comfortable *rôtisseries* where chicken is broiled on a spit, then served with Belgian fried potatoes and applesauce. There are pastry shops where the French *pâtisseries* are made twice as rich as in France, where the chocolates are succulent.

In the Bois de la Cambre, Brussels' Central Park, tea gardens dispense thick, hot chocolate with a speck of cinnamon, and *cramique,* a rich raisin bread baked in eight-pound loaves. This is the gastronome's paradise, where he can dine in elegant restaurants in the style of Brillat-Savarin or rest his *foie* on the simple fare of the provinces or sit in quaint cafés or ale houses such as *La Fleur en Papier Doré, L'Image Notre-Dame, Le Nez qui Pend, La Jambe de Bois* with rowdy students from Brussels University, or more peacefully, watch the archery guilds on Sunday afternoon practice in the *Jardin aux Fleurs,* shooting at parrots' feathers impaled on a tall pole. There, with a tall glass of Gueuze or Faro or Kriek Lambic, highly fermented beers which acquire dignity with old age like vintage wine, one can get from the pushcart vendors nearby a main order of tiny crabs, miniature steamed snails called *karicollen,* French fried potatoes prosaically served in brown paper bags; one can eat *pottekees,* a variety of pot cheese fermented with chopped onion in an earthen crock, spread on a thick slice of brown bread with scallions to enhance its flavor. There is nothing more delicious with a glass of *bière d'Orval.* Nothing more restful either than the jolly atmosphere of those cafés with a literary tradition which contrasts sharply with the chromium bars and neon lights of modernistic cafés on the boulevards and the Place de Brouckère. For Brussels, like all of Belgium, is at once a place of the past and of the future.

Pot Herb Soup

- *Soupe Verte*

  1 cup green peas
  1 leek, sliced
  2 cans chicken broth
  1 shallot, sliced
  Few sprigs chives
  Handful each of fresh parsley, sorrel, chervil
  ½ cup thick Béchamel Sauce (see Index)
  2 egg yolks beaten with ¼ cup heavy cream
  Pepper and salt to taste

Wash leek under stream of cold water to remove mud between the leaves. Cook peas and leek in broth until tender. Meanwhile place all vegetables in wooden bowl and chop *very* fine. Blend broth with Béchamel and egg yolk-cream mixture. Thicken by bringing to boiling point. Remove from heat. Taste and correct seasoning. Makes 6 cups.

Cream of Endive Soup

- *Crème Brabançonne*

  1 lb. endive
  5 cups chicken stock
  ⅛ tsp. cayenne pepper
  1 cup thick Béchamel Sauce (see Index)
  1 beef bouillon cube
  3 egg yolks
  2 tbsp. heavy cream

Wash endive and trim root ends. Cook until very tender, about 20 minutes, in chicken stock to which pepper has been added. Remove endive from broth and press through a food mill. Return to broth. Add Béchamel Sauce and bouillon cube and bring to a boil, stirring until bouillon cube is dissolved. Add egg yolks which have been beaten with cream, stirring until soup thickens. Do not boil. Remove from heat immediately. Serves 6.

Scrambled Eggs Tricolor

• *Oeufs Brouillés Tricolores*

(The Belgian colors are black, yellow and red)

> 2 tomatoes, sliced
> 6 tbsp. butter
>   Pepper and salt to taste
> 8 eggs
> 1 small can truffle peelings
> 1 tbsp. heavy cream
> 8 slices trimmed white toast

Slice tomatoes. Melt and heat 3 tablespoons of the butter to sizzling point in skillet. Sauté tomato slices in it. Season, with accent on the pepper. Reserve.

Melt remaining 3 tablespoons butter in top of a double boiler. Bring to sizzling point. Break eggs into it. Add truffle peelings and stir gently until a glossy mixture is formed. Remove double boiler from heat and add heavy cream. Continue to stir while pouring over the toast slices. Garnish with reserved tomatoes. Dust with pepper. Serves 4.

Eggs Belle-Aurore

• *Oeufs Belle-Aurore*

4 eggs
1 tbsp. tomato paste
1 cup Béchamel Sauce made with consommé (see Index)
2 tbsp. paprika
Salt to taste

Butter 4 small individual ovenproof cups. Break one egg into each. Place cups in a flat pan containing a small amount of water. Coddle eggs 5 minutes over low heat; cover and cook for five minutes more.

Add tomato paste to cream sauce. Mix in paprika and salt. Remove eggs from molds; cover with sauce. Serve hot, with toast. Serves 4.

Brussels Fondue

• *Fondue Bruxelloise*

1 cup grated cheese (half Swiss, half Italian)
2 cups very heavy Béchamel Sauce (see Index. Double flour and butter)
Pepper and salt to taste
3 egg yolks
1 egg beaten with 1 tsp. cooking oil
½ cup toasted bread crumbs

Allow grated cheese to melt in Béchamel Sauce. Season to taste. Remove sauce from heat and add egg yolks, stirring constantly. Spread mixture in oblong dish. Cool. Shape like codfish cakes.

Roll cakes in beaten egg and oil mixture, then in bread crumbs. Fry in deep fat (390°) until golden brown. Serve piping hot as a first course. Makes 8 fondues. This same recipe may be used to make "Cheese Délicieuses," tiny round cheese balls served on toothpicks as an appetizer at cocktail parties.

Mussels Marinière

- *Moules Marinières*

(As familiar to any Belgian as Boston baked beans to an American)

    10 qts. mussels in the shells
     3 celery stalks, diced
     2 onions, sliced
     2 shallots, minced
     4 sprigs parsley, chopped
     1 clove garlic, crushed
     6 slices lemon
       Pepper and a little salt

Scrub mussels and wash them thoroughly in warm water. In a large pot place vegetables, lemon and seasonings with ¼ cup boiling water. Cook until vegetables are tender.

Add mussels, cover kettle and steam for 15 minutes, shaking pot occasionally, or until all mussels are open.

Serve in the broth with side dish of Fried Potatoes (see Index) and pickles. Serves 5.

Mock Snails

- *Moules à l'Escargot*

Prepare 1 day ahead

> 3 qts. mussels
> 1 cup Court-Bouillon (see Index)
> 4 slices bacon
> 1 clove garlic

STUFFING:

> 1 tbsp. chopped parsley
> 1 tsp. dried chervil
> 2 shallots
> 4 cloves garlic
> 1 slice raw bacon, minced finely
> Juice of 1 lemon
> Pepper and salt to taste
> ¼ lb. butter, softened

Scrub mussels and rinse several times until warm water is clear of sand. Then steam with Court-Bouillon, bacon and garlic until all shells are open.

Meanwhile prepare stuffing by blending all ingredients into butter and working into a smooth paste.

Discard top half shell and remove mussel from the other half. Reserve. Place a little stuffing in each shell, replace mussel in it and cover with more stuffing. Place in baking dish; store overnight in refrigerator.

Preheat oven to 350° and bake 5 minutes. Serve at once with crusty French bread, *un*buttered. Serves 4, generously, as a first course.

Eels with Pot Herbs

• *Anguilles au Vert*

>   2 lbs. eels cut in 2-in. sections
>   2 tbsp. butter
>   ½ cup dry white wine
>   1 tbsp. minced chives
>   2 tsp. minced shallot, scallion or onion
>   ⅛ tsp. chopped fresh or dried sage
>   1 tbsp. chopped parsley
>   ⅛ tsp. tarragon, chopped or powdered
>   ⅛ tsp. savory, chopped or dried
>   1 tsp. chervil, chopped or dried
>   2 egg yolks, beaten

In a deep skillet sauté eel sections in butter and brown lightly on both sides. Add wine plus enough water to cover. Add herbs and seasonings. Simmer covered until fish can easily be removed from the bone (about 7 minutes). Stir egg in sauce, allowing to thicken without boiling. Taste and correct seasoning. Serve hot as a first course. This dish freezes very well and serves 4 generously.

For a cold hors d'oeuvre remove fish from sauce. Soak ½ envelope unflavored gelatin according to package directions. Dilute it with a little water and add to the sauce. Place fish in individual molds, cover with the sauce and allow to set in refrigerator. Unmold on a bed of lettuce.

Chicken Pâté

- *Pâté Bruxellois*

    1 fricassee chicken (5 to 6 lbs.)
    1 recipe Court-Bouillon (see Index)
    2 lbs. chopped pork (on the fatty side)
      Pepper and salt to taste
    ⅛ tsp. powdered thyme
    ⅛ tsp. powdered basil
    ⅛ tsp. powdered savory
    ½ cup brandy or sherry
    1 bay leaf

Poach chicken in Court-Bouillon for 20 minutes. Drain. Remove skin. Carve white meat in thick slices and reserve. Remove all other meat from carcass, grind, then pound to a smooth paste in mortar together with pork. Place in a bowl with seasonings and wine. Blend. Line an ovenproof *pâté* casserole (not Pyrex) or 3 coffee cans with slices of fat back, then put a layer of meat paste in the bottom of casserole. Wrap white meat filets in fat back and place filet in center of casserole. Cover with another layer of meat paste. Top with bay leaf and slices of fat back. Cover casserole or cans, place in a pan of water and bake in hot oven (400°) 2 hours.

This *pâté* will keep in a cool place as long as top layer of fat remains undisturbed.

Serve cold with Mayonnaise (see Index) and green salad.

Breast of Chicken Suprême

- *Médaillons de Volaille*

> 8 pieces breast of chicken
> 2 celery stalks
> 1 leek
> 1 carrot
> ½ bay leaf
> ⅛ tsp. thyme
> 3 cups Sauce Suprême

Poach chicken until tender in just enough water to cover, with vegetables and seasonings. Meanwhile, prepare:

SAUCE SUPRÊME:

> 1 can brushed truffles
> 2 cups medium Béchamel Sauce (see Index), made with chicken broth
> 4 tbsp. butter
> 1 cup heavy cream
> Dusting cayenne pepper
> Pepper and salt to taste
> 1 tsp. brandy

Reserve liquid in can of truffles. Peel truffles. Incorporate peelings into boiling Béchamel. Remove from heat. Slice truffles into a small pan. Add liquid from can and cook 1 minute. Season with pepper and salt. Add brandy, set aflame and shake pan gently over heat for 1 more minute. Reserve truffles.

When chicken is done, remove skin from the chicken breasts, arrange them on heated platter. Pour sauce over them. Decorate with slices of brandied truffles.

Chicken on the Spit

- *Poulet Rôti à la Broche*

Roast chicken in rotisserie. When done, serve with tart applesauce, fried potatoes and watercress.

Quick Chicken en Gelée

- *Poulet en Gelée*

    1 can jellied chicken consommé
    ¼ cup cognac or good port wine
    1 can truffles, sliced (optional)
    1 broiler
    1 tbsp. butter
    Pepper and salt to taste
    2 slices boiled ham
    ½ cup each cooked peas and carrots, drained
    1 celery heart, chopped, cooked and drained
    Parsley, lettuce and tomatoes

Warm consommé slightly, add cognac and truffle liquid to it. Season to taste. Allow to set a little in ice compartment of refrigerator. Meanwhile, wash and dry chicken. Place it, skin side down, in broiling pan. Add butter, pepper and salt. Broil 15 minutes at 350°. Turn chicken and raise temperature to 375°. Broil for 15 more minutes, basting from time to time. Allow chicken to cool in refrigerator. Cut in four pieces.

Cut slices of boiled ham in half. Arrange them on a platter with some parsley and lettuce leaves and sliced tomatoes. On each piece of ham put a piece of chicken. Arrange truffles, peas, carrots and chopped celery heart in designs on and around chicken. When consommé is partly set, spread a coating of it on the pieces of chicken and vegetables with pastry brush. Glaze in refrigerator for 2 hours before serving. Serves 4.

Chicken 1928

- *Poulet 1928* *

> 2 fryers, cut up
> 6 tbsp. butter
> 1 pair sweetbreads blanched 10 minutes in warm water
> ½ lb. mushrooms, sliced
> 1 small can truffles
> ¼ cup port wine
> Pepper and salt to taste
> Dusting of cayenne pepper
> ½ cup grated imported Swiss cheese
> 3 cups light Béchamel Sauce (see Index) made with chicken broth to which are added pan juices from the cooking of truffles, mushrooms and sweetbreads
> ½ cup dry bread crumbs mixed with 2 tbsp. grated Parmesan cheese
> Dots of butter

Sauté chicken in 2 tablespoons of the butter, more or less, until golden brown. Cover and simmer in their own juice for 15 minutes. Reserve.

Meanwhile, slice sweetbreads horizontally and sauté with mushrooms over medium heat in remaining butter. Reserve.

Slice truffles thinly and cook 2 minutes over medium heat in small pan with port and liquor from the can.

In heavily buttered casserole pack chicken pieces side by

* From the year a friend of mine tossed it up and brought it to the table with a *sweet* white wine, a remarkable *Château Yquem.*

side. Season. Sprinkle with ½ of the Swiss cheese, top with mushrooms and sweetbreads and sprinkle with rest of cheese. Finish with sliced truffles, then pour sauce over all. Sprinkle with cheese-bread crumb mixture, dot with butter and bake uncovered in medium oven (350°) 25 minutes.

Serves 6 gourmets comfortably—only 4 gourmands.

Breast of Chicken Brabançonne

- *Médaillons de Volaille Brabançonne*

        4 to 6 chicken breasts
            1 carrot
            1 stalk celery
            ½ bay leaf
              Pepper and salt to taste
            8 stalks endive
              Juice of 1 lemon
            4 tbsp. butter
            1 jigger cognac more or less

Poach chicken in 2 cups water with carrot, celery, bay leaf, pepper and salt. Remove chicken and reserve broth for other uses. Bring endive to a boil in 2 quarts water; reduce heat, add lemon juice. Simmer for 20 minutes. Pour off liquid from endive but do not drain completely. Place in skillet or flameproof casserole with butter and chicken and braise over medium to high heat until edges of vegetables and meat are lightly browned. Taste and correct seasoning.

Warm cognac slightly. Bring casserole to the table. Ignite cognac and pour into casserole. Serves 4.

Squab en Casserole *

• *Pigeons en Casserole*

> 4 squabs
> Pepper and salt to taste
> ¼ lb. butter
> 8 juniper berries
> ½ cup Burgundy wine
> 1 slice bacon
> ¼ lb. butter (more or less)
> 4 slices white bread, trimmed

Wash and dry squabs. Rub with pepper and salt. Reserve livers. Melt ¼ pound butter in flameproof casserole. Place squabs in casserole. Brown on all sides. Add berries, wine and bacon. Cover and cook over slow heat for half an hour.

Meanwhile, melt one-half of the remaining ¼ pound butter in frying pan, place slices of bread in it, fry to golden brown on both sides, adding more butter when necessary. Reserve. Sauté livers in the same pan in the leftover butter. Pound them to a paste. Spread paste on croutons. Slip croutons under birds and serve from casserole.

---

* In our family, squab was a must on Easter Day. It was served, a half to each guest, as a trifle after the roast, which came after the fish, which came after the soup, which came after the hors d'oeuvres.

Duck Brussels Style

- *Canard à la Bruxelloise*

    1 duckling
    3 slices bacon, cut thick and diced
    1 pair sweetbreads, diced
    1 tbsp. butter
    Pepper and salt to taste
    ½ tbsp. parsley, chopped
    ½ tbsp. chives, chopped
    2 tbsp. canned mushrooms (stems and pieces), chopped
    ½ cup dry white wine
    1 carrot
    2 medium-sized onions
    1 tbsp. flour
    1 tbsp. butter

Wash and dry duck, inside and out. Stuff it with diced bacon and sweetbreads mixed with one tablespoon butter, pepper and salt, and chopped herbs and mushrooms. Truss carefully and put bird in open roasting pan with white wine, carrot and onions.

Roasting should take about 1½ hours in hot oven (475°). When done, remove duck to heated platter. Strain gravy. Remove extra fat from pan drippings and boil down to about half the original quantity, then taste and correct seasoning. For thickening use one tablespoon flour kneaded with a tablespoon of butter. Give sauce a final boil to avoid taste of flour.

Disjoint duck and arrange pieces over stuffing on a heated platter. Garnish with carrots, peas, cauliflower and fried potato balls. Serves 4.

Duck Congolese

• *Canard de Matadi*

> 1 No. 2 can whole peeled apricots
> 1 duck, 5 to 6 lbs.
> 1 apple
> 1 stalk celery
> Pepper and salt to taste
> 1 cup stock or canned chicken broth
> 2 tbsp. butter kneaded with 2 tbsp. flour

Drain apricots, warm slowly to garnish duck and reserve 1 cup of the nectar.

Dry duck inside and out. Place apple and celery in cavity with pepper and salt. Season lightly and roast uncovered for 1½ hours in 450° oven. Remove duck from pan; keep warm on a hot platter.

Skim or pour off all fat in pan. Deglaze pan with chicken broth, drop butter-flour mixture into the pan, add apricot nectar and allow to boil until reduced to ⅔ original volume (about 7 to 8 minutes) stirring occasionally.

Meanwhile, discard apple and celery. Carve duck into 6 pieces. Replace on platter, garnish with apricots and pour sauce over all. Serve with toast points and a crisp bowl of unseasoned watercress. Serves 4.

Sweet Potatoes Congolese

- *Beignets de Patates Douces*

      4 medium-sized sweet potatoes
      ¼ cup honey
      ¼ cup brandy
      1 tsp. grated lemon rind

FRITTER BATTER:

      2 cups flour
      1 pt. light beer

Blend flour and beer until a smooth paste is obtained.

Blanch sweet potatoes 5 minutes in boiling water. Peel and slice them. Marinate them 1 hour in honey-brandy-lemon rind mixture. Without drying slices, dip them in batter. Fry in deep fat (390°) until golden brown. Serve very hot. Serves 4.

These fritters are excellent with roast turkey.

Flemish Beer Stew

- *Carbonnade Flamande*

      1 lb. onions, thinly sliced
      4 tbsp. butter
    2½ lbs. round steak, cubed
      1 clove garlic, pressed or crushed
      ⅛ tsp. nutmeg
      ⅛ tsp. thyme
        Pepper and salt to taste
      1 qt. light beer
      2 tbsp. butter kneaded with 2 tbsp. flour
      1 tbsp. granulated sugar

Sauté onions lightly in 2 tablespoons of the butter in deep pan or flameproof casserole. Reserve. In same pot melt remaining butter and brown beef on all sides until it has a *very* dark color. When done, replace onions, add seasonings, then beer. Cover, bring to a boil, reduce heat and simmer for 1½ hours. Remove meat from pan juices and keep hot. Drop butter-flour mixture into juices, add sugar and boil uncovered for 8 minutes over medium heat. Taste, correct seasoning.

Serve with boiled potatoes and drink beer with this delectable dish. Serves 4.

Choesels with Madeira

(Pronounced "shoosels")

        1 oxtail, cut in pieces
        2 cups bacon drippings
        3 sprigs parsley
       ¼ tsp. thyme
        1 bay leaf
          Salt, pepper, cayenne pepper
        2 calves brains
        2 lbs. breast of veal
        2 medium onions, sliced
        1 beef kidney, peeled and diced
       ¼ cup pale ale
        1 pancreas of beef
        1 sweetbread, blanched and sliced
        1 quart pale ale
        1 cup cooked mushrooms
        1 jar calves feet in jelly
        2 tsp. cornstarch
        1 cup Madeira wine

Preparation of this dish necessitates a lot of work. Belgian women make it in large quantities. It can be frozen easily or keeps in the refrigerator for about six days. Reheat in double boiler.

Brown oxtail in drippings slowly. Add herbs and season rather highly. Add calves brains and simmer slowly for 15 minutes. Add breast of veal and sliced onions. Cook together slowly for ½ hour. Add pieces of kidney. When these are stiff, moisten with ¼ cup of ale. Season. Cook for 15 minutes. Then add the choesels (pancreas) and sweetbreads. Add quart of ale and the mushrooms. Cook for another 10 minutes.

Lastly, cut calves feet in half and add with jelly. Cook 15 minutes more. Remove meats to a deep casserole or platter. Keep hot. Allow sauce to come to a boil. Correct seasoning and, if necessary, thicken with 2 teaspoons cornstarch diluted in some water, and pour in the Madeira. Check seasoning.

Cover meats with sauce and serve with a side dish of boiled potatoes or a green vegetable. Regardless of chi-chi, you should sop up the sauce with a slice of buttered brown bread! Serves 12.

Lamb Ragoût Brabançonne

- *Ragoût de Mouton aux Chicons*

    8 shoulder lamb chops, trimmed
    2 lbs. Belgian endive
    1 medium-sized onion, chopped
    1 clove garlic, minced or crushed
    1 bay leaf
    ½ tsp. powdered thyme
    ⅛ tsp. powdered clove
    1 sprig parsley
    Pepper and salt to taste
    1 cup beef consommé

Place lamb chops standing on their fatty edge in bottom of large flameproof casserole. Render some of the fat over medium heat. Lay the chops down, then brown them rapidly over high heat on both sides. Carefully skim all fat from drippings. Place washed endive in bottom of casserole, add vegetables, seasoning and consommé.

Place chops in center of vegetables. Cover and simmer over low heat for ½ hour. Remove meat and vegetables to a hot platter. Keep warm in the oven. Taste and correct seasoning if necessary. Boil juices down over high heat until reduced to half the volume. Pour juice over ragout and serve with plain boiled potatoes.

Belgian Veal Blanquette

- *Blanquette de Veau*

2 lbs. breast of veal, cut for stew
3 tbsp. butter
1 cup beef consommé
⅛ tsp. thyme
1 bay leaf
12 shallots *or* 12 scallions, bulb end only
⅛ tsp. nutmeg
　Salt and pepper to taste
½ lb. ground veal
½ lb. ground pork
½ cup crumbs from fresh bread
¼ cup milk
1 egg
2 tbsp. butter
12 mushroom caps
2 tbsp. flour
1½ cups consommé
2 egg yolks
　Juice of half a lemon

In a flameproof casserole lightly brown pieces of veal in butter. Moisten with consommé and add herbs, shallots and nutmeg. Season to taste. Add water to cover. Bring to a boil. Reduce heat and allow to simmer over low heat for 1 hour in covered pan.

In the meantime, place chopped pork, chopped veal, bread crumbs, milk and egg in a bowl. Mix all together and roll into tiny meat balls the size of a nut. Sauté in butter with mushroom caps. Add to stew. Bring to a boil. Reduce heat and allow to simmer.

In a saucepan melt leftover butter, add flour and blend, stirring briskly. Moisten with consommé and allow to thicken. Add to stew and simmer all together 15 minutes. Remove from fire. Bind with 2 egg yolks and stir in lemon juice.

Serve hot with rice or mashed potatoes.

Veal Loaf Brussels Style

• *Pain de Veau*

> 2 lbs. ground veal
> 2 lbs. ground pork
> ¼ cup finely chopped onion
> 1 tbsp. finely chopped parsley
> ½ cup bread crumbs
> 1 tbsp. heavy cream or evaporated milk
> 2 eggs
> 2 tbsp. salt
> ¼ tsp. pepper
> ⅛ tsp. nutmeg
> 2 tbsp. flour
> ⅛ lb. butter
> ½ cup white wine

Mix in a deep dish the veal, pork, onion, parsley, bread crumbs, cream and eggs. Season to taste.

Mold into loaf. Roll in flour. Butter the bottom of an oven-proof baking dish and place the veal loaf in it. Cover with dabs of butter. Bake in hot oven (475°) for 1½ hours.

A few minutes before it is done, pour wine over the veal loaf and mix into the pan drippings. Serves 6.

Stuffed Tomatoes

• *Tomates Farcies aux Fricadelles*

> 8 medium tomatoes
> 1 tsp. salt
> ½ lb. veal *or* leftover meat, ground
> 1 egg
> 2 tbsp. bread crumbs
> 2 tbsp. butter
> 1 small onion, chopped
> 1 tsp. chopped parsley
> ¼ tsp. basil
>   Salt, pepper and nutmeg to taste
> 2 tbsp. heavy cream

Cut *top* slice off tomatoes. Carefully remove liquid, seeds and the inner part of tomatoes. Reserve. Sprinkle a little salt in each shell.

Mix chopped meat, egg, bread crumbs and seasoning in a bowl. Carefully empty shells of any liquid drawn by salt. Fill tomato shells with mixture. Cover with top slices. Dot with 1 tablespoon of the butter. Bake 20 minutes in moderate oven (350°).

Meanwhile simmer the reserved part of tomatoes with 1 tablespoon of the butter, onion, parsley, basil, nutmeg, salt and pepper, for 10 minutes. Strain. Reheat and boil briskly until sauce is reduced to half its quantity. Add cream. Taste and correct seasoning.

Pour over the tomatoes. Serve with mashed potatoes and a green vegetable. Serves 4.

Witloof or Belgian Endive au Gratin

- *Chicons au gratin*

  8 heads witloof
  4 slices ham
  2 cups Béchamel Sauce (see Index)
  ½ lb. grated Switzerland Swiss cheese
  ¼ cup white wine
  1 tbsp. bread crumbs
  1 tbsp. butter

Witloof, according to individual taste, can be boiled in a large quantity of water or, to preserve its characteristic bitter flavor, it can be smothered.

If boiled, the cooking time is from 20 to 25 minutes. If smothered—that is, cooked in about 1 cup of water with butter, salt and pepper over a low flame—it will take about an hour.

Drain witloof, press to force out all the cooking liquid, which would dilute the cheese sauce. Roll each head of witloof in half a slice of ham. Place the rolls on a shallow baking dish. Cover with Béchamel Sauce in which the grated cheese has been melted and the white wine added. Sprinkle with bread crumbs and add little dabs of butter. Brown under the broiler. Serves 4.

Sweetbreads with Scotch Whisky Sauce

• *Ris de Veau au Whisky*

> 2 pairs sweetbreads
> ¼ cup flour (more or less)
> Salt and pepper to taste
> 1 egg beaten with 1 tsp. salad oil
> ½ cup bread crumbs (more or less)
> ¼ lb. butter
> 1 cup Béchamel Sauce (see Index)
> 1 egg yolk beaten with 2 tbsp. heavy cream
> 1 tsp. tomato purée
> 2 tbsp. Scotch whisky
> 2 tomatoes, sliced
> 2 tbsp. butter
> 1 tsp. chopped parsley

Soak sweetbreads in lukewarm water for 10 minutes. Divide into natural pieces without cutting. Remove white membrane which held the pieces together. Do *not* peel sweetbreads. Place flour and seasoning into brown paper bag. Drop sweetbreads into bag. Shake until well coated with flour. Dip into beaten egg mixture, then roll in bread crumbs. Melt butter over high heat in a skillet. When butter sizzles drop the sweetbreads into it and sauté until golden brown on both sides. Add 2 tablespoons water to juices in skillet. Cover. Reduce heat to low and simmer 10 minutes longer.

Meanwhile, make Béchamel Sauce and add egg yolk mixture to it. Dilute tomato purée with Scotch, mix into sauce. Taste and correct seasoning. Keep hot in double boiler, stirring one in a while.

Sauté sliced tomatoes gently in 2 tablespoons butter over medium heat for 2 minutes.

Place sweetbreads in center of preheated platter. Surround with tomato slices. Pour sauce over sweetbreads, leaving the edges of tomatoes showing. Garnish with chopped parsley. Serve with green peas.

Serves 4 as first course, 2 as entree.

Fricadellen

• *Fricadelles*

>   1 lb. ground veal
>   1 lb. ground pork
>   ½ lb. ground beef
>   3 slices white bread, trimmed
>   2 eggs, whole
>   4 tbsp. milk
>   Salt and pepper to taste
>   ⅛ tsp. nutmeg
>   ¼ lb. butter
>   1 small can tomato paste
>   ¼ cup beef broth
>   4 tbsp. heavy cream

Place meats in bowl. Crumble white bread over the meats, add eggs and milk. Season to taste. Add nutmeg. Mix thoroughly. Roll into balls. Sauté in butter. When brown, add tomato paste, beef broth and simmer for 15 minutes.

Remove meat balls to a preheated platter. Correct seasoning and consistency of the sauce—either add liquid to it or reduce it over high heat. Then add cream. Pour over meat balls and serve with mashed potatoes.

Veal Chop with Sorrel

- *Côte de Veau à l'Oseille*

>   3 tbsp. butter
>   3 ribs of veal cut as *one* chop
>   Pepper and salt to taste
>   ¼ lb. fresh sorrel
>   ½ cup heavy cream

Melt butter in flameproof casserole. Brown chop on both sides; reduce heat. Season with pepper and salt, cover and simmer until tender.

Meanwhile pull leafy part from stems of sorrel and wash thoroughly. Remove chop from casserole and keep hot. Place sorrel in casserole. Cover. Cook over medium heat 5 minutes. Add cream and stir until a thick green sauce is obtained. Taste and correct seasoning.

Replace chop on bed of sorrel and serve with boiled potatoes. Serves 2 to 3.

Potatoes Bruxelloise

- *Pommes de Terres à la Bruxelloise*

>   6 medium-sized potatoes
>   6 leeks
>   Pepper and salt to taste
>   ¼ lb. Swiss cheese, grated
>   ¼ lb. butter
>   ½ cup scalded milk
>   ½ pt. heavy cream

Slice potatoes as for potato chips. Cut leeks in small roundels. Place alternate layers of potatoes and leeks in a heavily buttered casserole. Season to taste. Dust with grated cheese. Dot with butter and over all pour scalded milk and heavy cream.

Bake in a moderate oven (350°) for approximately ¾ hour, or until well browned on top. Serves 6.

Fried Potatoes

• *Pommes Frites*

6 large potatoes

Peel and wash potatoes. Cut them in sticks the size of your little finger. Dry them *thoroughly* in a towel.

Have a large pot of smoking fat for frying (suet, oil or vegetable shortening, according to taste). To make sure fat is at correct temperature, throw in a bread crust. It should come to the surface immediately and start browning, but not burning.

Place potato sticks in wire basket and dip them in deep fat until pale yellow. Remove, cool for half an hour and repeat procedure until potatoes are golden brown.

Remove wire basket. Shake potatoes in brown paper bag to drain extra fat and serve piping hot, sprinkled with salt.

Fried potatoes are sold from pushcarts at street corners in Belgium and are eaten right out of the bag, like chestnuts.

They are always on the menu with *bifteck* (which is not steak) and with Mussels Marinière (see Index).

Brussels Sprouts in Celery Sauce

• *Choux de Bruxelles au Celeri*

> 4 packages frozen Brussels sprouts
> 2 cups chopped celery
> 2 cups beef broth or stock

Cook sprouts in boiling salted water until tender. Drain. At the same time in another pot cook celery in broth diluted with 1 cup boiling water. Reserve drained celery and use liquid to make

> 2 cups Béchamel Sauce (see Index) seasoned with celery salt and grated nutmeg

In this sauce place celery and Brussels sprouts. Stir, taste. correct seasoning and heat vegetables through and through over *low* heat and before serving. Serves 6.

Brussels Sprouts au Gratin

• *Choux de Bruxelles Gratinés*

> 2 cups chicken consommé or stock
> 2 packages frozen Brussels sprouts *or* 1 qt. fresh
> ⅛ tsp. nutmeg
> Pepper to taste
> 2 cups Béchamel Sauce (see Index) made with liquid in which sprouts were cooked
> ½ cup Switzerland Swiss cheese, grated
> 2 tbsp. dry white wine
> ½ cup dry bread crumbs
> Dots of butter

Bring consommé to a boil. Add sprouts, nutmeg and pepper and simmer 15 minutes, or until done. Drain and keep hot. Make Béchamel Sauce with sprout liquid. Over medium heat melt cheese in the sauce, stirring often. Add white wine.

Place hot sprouts in baking dish. Cover with sauce. Sprinkle with bread crumbs. Dot with butter. Place under the broiler until golden brown.

Serve with pan-fried slices of Canadian bacon. Serves 4.

Brussels Sprouts with Chestnuts

- *Choux de Bruxelles aux Marrons*

     1 No. 2 can chestnuts
     3 packages frozen Brussels sprouts
     2 tbsp. butter
     ⅛ tsp. nutmeg
       Salt and pepper to taste

Drain canned chestnuts. Reserve ¼ cup of their liquor. Cook Brussels sprouts and drain them well. Add butter and chestnuts and reserved liquor. Reheat, simmer for 5 minutes, dusting with nutmeg.

Serve very hot with pork or turkey. Serves 6.

Braised Endive

- *Chicons Braisés*

     1½ lbs. Belgian endive
       Juice of ½ lemon
     3 tbsp. butter
       Pepper and salt to taste

Boil endive in a large quantity of salted water for 18 minutes, adding lemon juice. Place endive and butter in heavy skillet or frying pan. Simmer, uncovered, over medium heat until liquid has completely evaporated and edges of vegetable take on a golden color. Season with pepper and salt. Serves 4.

Alice Salad

• *Salade Alice*

> 4 apples
> 1 cup water mixed with 2 tbsp. lemon juice
> 1 celery heart
> ½ banana
> ½ cup sour cream
> 1 tsp. lemon juice
> ½ tsp. salt
> 2 stalks Belgian endive

Peel and core apples. Soak in water-lemon juice mixture 10 minutes to prevent apples from discoloring. Cut a ring from top of apple to make a cover.

Hollow out the apple. Chop apple meat with celery and banana. Mix with cream, lemon juice and salt. Replace inside the apple. In center stick 2 or 3 leaves of endive. Slide cover over endive so that the leaves protrude through the ring. Serve chilled. Serves 4.

Each apple makes an individual salad.

Field Salad with Endive *

• *Salade de Blé*

>   4 stalks Belgian endive
> 1/4 lb. field salad
> 1/4 head red cabbage, cored and shredded
>   1 cup Mayonnaise (see Index) highly seasoned

Wash and thoroughly drain vegetables. Cut endive into 1-inch chunks and divide. Place endive in bottom of salad bowl. Make a feathery ring around edge of bowl with field salad. Toward center make a ring of red cabbage and drop Mayonnaise in center.

Toss at the table. Serves 4 to 6.

Salad Brabançonne

• *Salade Brabançonne*

>   8 stalks Belgian endive
>   1 cup Mayonnaise (see Index) highly seasoned, mixed
>   with 1 tsp. prepared English mustard
>   1 red apple, cored and diced

Cut endive into 1-inch chunks. Wash and thoroughly drain. Divide. Mix with Mayonnaise and half the apple.

Place in glass salad bowl. Decorate around the rim with remaining apple cubes, red peel showing. Serves 4.

* Called *Roquette* in the South. *Doucette* in Liége.

Lemon Mousse

- *Mousse au Citron*

> 1 qt. milk (reserve ½ cup)
> ½ cup granulated sugar
> 1 tbsp. cornstarch
> 6 egg yolks
> 3 egg whites
> 1 tsp. lemon extract

Place milk and sugar in saucepan over high heat and bring to a boil. Meanwhile, dissolve cornstarch in reserved cold milk and add egg yolks.

As soon as milk in saucepan boils pour in the cold mixture, stirring rapidly. Allow to thicken until it coats the spoon well. Remove from heat and allow to cool a little.

Beat egg whites until foamy but not stiff. Fold egg whites and lemon extract into the custard. Pour into mold and chill. Serve very cold. Serves 6.

Rum Chipolata

- *Chipolata au Rhum*

> 1 qt. milk (reserve ½ cup)
> ½ cup granulated sugar
> 1 tbsp. cornstarch
> 6 egg yolks
> 3 egg whites
> 3 tbsp. rum
> 8 medium-sized macaroons *or* lady fingers, sprinkled
>   with ¼ cup rum and water combined
> 1 tbsp. unsweetened chocolate, grated

Proceed as for Lemon Mousse (see Index), substituting 3 tablespoons rum for lemon extract. Line serving bowl with rum-sprinkled macaroons or lady fingers. Pour in pudding and grate unsweetened chocolate over top. Chill. Serves 6.

White Maiden with a Red Heart

- *Blanche Neige et Rouge Vermeille*

     3 tbsp. cornstarch
     1 qt. milk
     ¼ cup granulated sugar
     ¼ cup grated almonds
     2 tsp. almond extract
     ½ cup raspberry jam

Dilute cornstarch in ½ cup cold milk. Scald remaining milk with sugar. At boiling point, pour in cornstarch mixture. Allow pudding to thicken, stirring constantly. Remove from heat and stir in almonds and extract. Cool a little.

Place jam in bowl and pour pudding over it. Chill thoroughly and serve. Serves 6.

Chocolate Mousse

- *Mousse au Chocolat*

     3 tbsp. Grand Marnier
     8 oz. semisweet chocolate
     6 egg yolks
     1 tsp. grated orange rind
     7 egg whites, beaten stiff

Place Grand Marnier in top of double boiler over hot water and melt chocolate in it. Add egg yolks and orange rind and stir until smooth. Fold chocolate into egg whites. Pour into demitasse cups or special French "petits pots." Allow to set 8 hours in refrigerator.

Serve with a Brussels Cookie (see following recipe). Makes 6 demitasse cups.

Brussels Cookies

- *Biscuits*

      4 cups all-purpose flour
      2 tsp. honey
      1 cup brown sugar, packed
      2 cups sweet butter, melted
      1 egg, whole
      1 tsp. soda
      1 tsp. cinnamon

Mix all ingredients in electric mixer for 5 minutes, or beat for 15 minutes by hand. Make a roll and keep in refrigerator several hours. Cut in ¼-inch slices and bake in medium oven (350°) until done, about 12 minutes. Makes about 60 cookies.

Bread Pudding

- *Pudding*

        ½ cup raisins
        ½ cup white raisins
        ½ cup currants
        8 Holland rusks
        4 egg yolks
        ½ cup dark brown sugar
        2 jiggers rum
        1 pt. milk, scalded
        1 cup assorted candied fruit, finely chopped
        ½ cup glacéed cherries
        4 egg whites, beaten
        2 tbsp. butter

Soak raisins and currants in boiling water and allow to become plump. Place rusks, egg yolks, sugar and 1 jigger of the rum in large mixing bowl. Pour in scalded milk and let it soak into rusks. Work with a fork till rusks form a smooth paste. Drain raisins and currents and add with candied fruit. Fold in egg whites.

Rub melon-shaped pudding mold heavily with butter. Pour mixture into it up to ½ inch from top. Cover. Place in pan filled with hot water up to 1 inch of rim of mold and steam for 2 hours.

Invert on platter. Warm slightly remaining jigger of rum. Pour into ladle, set it aflame and pour over pudding. Serve with an American rum-flavored hard sauce. Serves 6.

Almond Bread Cookies

• *Pain d'Amandes*

> 4½ cups flour
> 1 tsp. double-action baking powder
> 1 tsp. cinnamon
> ⅛ tsp. salt
> 2 cups almonds, grated
> 1 cup whole blanched almonds
> 1¼ cup brown sugar
> ⅓ cup cognac plus 1 tbsp.
> ½ lb. butter, melted

Sift flour, baking powder, cinnamon and salt in a mixing bowl. Add grated and whole almonds and brown sugar. Pour in cognac and butter. Mix thoroughly with the hands until batter feels like clay. Shape into a roll. Wrap in waxed paper. Chill in refrigerator.

Slice cookies ¼-inch thick and place on buttered baking sheet. Bake in quick moderate oven (375°) for 10 minutes. Remove from pan immediately. Cool on wire rack. Makes about 60 cookies.

Spice Cookies *

- *Speculoos*

        4 cups flour
        1 tsp. cinnamon
        ½ tsp. double-action baking powder
        ½ tsp. nutmeg
        ¼ lb. sweet butter
     1¼ cups dark brown sugar
        1 egg
        ⅛ cup water

Sift flour, cinnamon and baking power together and add nutmeg. Cream butter and add sugar gradually. Beat egg well and blend into creamed mixture. Add dry ingredients gradually, alternating with water. Shape batter like a roll. Wrap in waxed paper and store in refrigerator until well chilled.

Roll out to ¼-inch thick on floured board. Cut with gingerbread man cutter. Bake on buttered baking sheet in a quick moderate oven (375°) for 12 minutes, or until evenly browned. Remove from pan quickly and cool on wire rack. Makes 20 to 24 cookies the size of a gingerbread man.

* These cookies are baked in the shape of St. Nicholas on December 6. Some are man size and are sold tied to a paper-wrapped board.

Beer Waffles *

- *Gaufres Bruxelloises*

    3½ cups flour
    ½ cup salad oil
    1½ pts. light beer
    ⅛ tsp. salt
    1 tbsp. Vanilla Sugar (see Index)
    2 eggs
    2 tbsp. grated lemon rind
    1 tsp. lemon juice

Place all ingredients in mixing bowl and blend to a smooth paste. Allow to rise slightly at room temperature for 2 hours.

Spread thinly on waffle iron so that waffle will be lacelike and crisp. These waffles brown quickly and should be served pale golden. Serve with sour cream and brown sugar. Makes 16 waffles.

Strawberries Bruxelloise

- *Fraises Bruxelloise*

    1 qt. strawberries
    3 tbsp. confectioners' sugar
    Juice of half a lemon
    ½ tsp. grated rind of an orange

Wash and hull strawberries and drain carefully. Mix sugar, lemon juice and orange rind. Cover the strawberries with this mixture. Chill in refrigerator. Serves 4.

* These waffles are served for dessert or tea. If wanted for breakfast, prepare the night before and store, unrisen, in refrigerator. Rising period unnecessary.

Apple Fritters *

- *Beignets de Pommes*

     2 cups flour
     1 pt. light beer
     4 apples, peeled, cored and sliced

Prepare batter by blending flour and beer to a paste. Dip each slice of apple in batter and fry in deep fat (390°) until golden brown. Drain on absorbent paper. Keep hot in oven.

Serve sprinkled with Vanilla Sugar (see Index) or with a light custard sauce. Serves 6.

Mandarin Torte

- *Tarte aux Mandarines*

     ¼ lb. plus 2 tbsp. butter
     ⅔ cup granulated sugar
     1 cup sifted flour
     1½ cups grated almonds
     1 tsp. grated lemon rind
     ⅛ tsp. cinnamon
     2 egg yolks
     1 hard-cooked egg yolk, sieved

FILLING: 3 cans mandarin orange sections, well-drained
     4 tbsp. orange marmalade
     1 tbsp. Grand Marnier

Place all ingredients for crust in a bowl and work with hands until it feels like modeling clay. Divide ¾ and ¼.

* These fritters are very light and crisp. The beer acts as a leavening and leaves no taste whatsoever. The best way to eat them is as fast as they come.

With fingers pat ¾ evenly on bottom of 9-inch springform pan. Pat remaining ¼ into an edge ½ inch high around sides of pan. Place mandarin sections side by side slightly overlapping each other, in a circle, until bottom of cake is entirely covered. Bake at 315° (325° is just a little too hot!) about 50 minutes. Do not brown.

Dilute orange marmalade with Grand Marnier, heat and pour evenly over fruit in cake. Serve cool.

Adèle's Ice Box Cake

- *Tôt-fait*

        1 lb. confectioners' sugar
        1 lb. sweet butter
      48 Petits-Beurres *or* Nabisco Social Tea Biscuits
        2 cups cold strong coffee (more or less)
       ½ cup cocoa

Cream powdered sugar and butter until white and very fluffy.

Dip sweet crackers in coffee and arrange 12 of them on a board to form a rectangle. Spread a layer of butter-sugar mixture over them, then sift a dusting of cocoa over this and cover with 12 more soaked crackers. Repeat 3 times. Finish with a coating of butter-sugar mixture on top and all sides. Dust with cocoa.

Place in refrigerator for 12 hours. Slice thinly. Serves 10 to 12.

Freezes perfectly. Thaw out at room temperature or overnight in refrigerator.

Hard Rolls

- *Pistolets*

½ cup lukewarm water (scant)
½ tbsp. sugar
½ tsp. salt
1 tbsp. melted butter
2 cups sifted all-purpose flour (more or less)
½ envelope dry yeast diluted in 4 tbsp. warm water
1 egg white, stiffly beaten

Measure water into mixing bowl, add sugar, salt, butter and ½ cup of the flour and beat until well blended. Add dissolved yeast, remaining flour and egg white and mix well. Turn dough onto lightly floured board and knead 6 minutes.

Place dough in a buttered bowl, butter top, and cover. Allow to rise in warm place for 1½ hours, or until double in bulk. Punch down dough and allow to rise a second time for about 45 minutes, or until doubled again.

Punch down and divide dough into 12 portions for the rolls. Shape each portion into a little loaf and cut a ½-inch gash in the middle. Place these pistolets 2½ inches apart on buttered baking sheet. Cover and let rise again 45 minutes. Bake in hot oven (450°) 20 minutes. Makes 1 dozen rolls.

For very crisp crusts, place a flat pan of boiling water on the bottom of the oven while baking.

Pistolets were introduced in Belgium at the time of Napoleon's conquest. The *pistole* was the dole given to the needy. The crusty breads were distributed free—hence their name.

Greek Bread

• *Pain à la Grecque*

    1 tsp. cinnamon sifted with 3 cups flour
    ½ cup sugar
    ½ envelope dry yeast diluted in 4 tbsp. warm water
    2 tbsp. honey
    1¾ cups lukewarm milk
    ½ lb. butter, melted
    Rock candy sugar

In a bowl sift ½ of dry ingredients. Add yeast, honey and milk and beat with spoon until well blended. Beat in butter. Add remaining dry ingredients, working with hands. Turn dough onto lightly floured board, cover and allow to stand 10 minutes. Knead 6 minutes. Shape round and allow to rise, covered, in a buttered bowl until double in bulk (about 2 hours).

Punch down dough. Roll out on floured board to ½-inch thickness, then cut into long strips 2½ inches wide. Dip these strips into sugar made from crushed rock candy. Lay far apart on buttered heavy baking sheets. Cover and let rise again for 30 minutes. Flatten out. Bake 15 minutes in moderate oven (350°) and cut into 7-inch pieces when they come out of the oven. Makes about 1½ dozen.

Rich Raisin Bread

• *Cramique*

> 1 cup raisins or currants
> 8 cups (2 lbs.) sifted flour
> 1/8 tsp. salt
> 1/4 cup lukewarm milk
> 1 package dry yeast dissolved in 1/4 cup warm water
> 3 egg yolks
> 1 tbsp. granulated sugar
> 3/4 cup butter, melted and cooled

Soak raisins or currants in hot water until plump.

Sift flour and salt into a large mixing bowl. Make a well in center and pour into it milk and dissolved yeast. Slowly work in half the flour from the sides. Let this dough stand 6 minutes. It will crack.

Blend in egg yolks, granulated sugar, butter and drained raisins. Knead into a loaf. Cover and let rise in warm place for 1 hour.

Punch down dough. Divide into 2 loaves and put into 2 well-buttered bread pans. Brush with beaten egg. Bake 15 minutes at 450°; then reduce heat to 350° and bake 20 to 30 minutes longer. When done, bread has a hollow sound when tapped and comes away from side of pan. Makes 2 loaves.

Most country inns serve this bread in the afternoon with coffee.

Index

Index

(The recipes are listed regionally on the contents page)